UNLEASH THE POWERS WITHIN

Q. *What did Goethe, Chopin, Tennyson, and Mozart have in common?*

A. *Each of these exceptional men is known to have used self-hypnosis as a creative tool.*

Indeed, many of the great financial success stories, medical discoveries, and works of influential inventors, artists, and writers have been attributed to the use of self-hypnosis to overcome creative obstacles and sharpen the powers of the mind. Now, with clear, simple, and easy-to-follow instructions, students, scholars, professional people, and anyone who wants to improve their concentration, sharpen memory, and raise their standards of achievement can learn to utilize this powerful natural gift we all possess.

POWER HYPNOSIS
*A Guide to Faster Learning
and Greater Self-Mastery*

POWER HYPNOSIS

A guide for faster learning and
greater self-mastery

(formerly titled: *Hypnosis and Power Learning*)

Pierre Clement

A SIGNET BOOK

NEW AMERICAN LIBRARY

A DIVISION OF PENGUIN BOOKS USA INC.

CONTENTS

2. OBJECTIVE: DISCOVERING YOUR OWN ELECTRONIC BRAIN

PART TWO: ACQUIRING SELF-HYPNOSIS

4. OBJECTIVE: DEEPENING AND TIMING HYPNOSIS

5. OBJECTIVE: ENTERTAINING YOURSELF AND "PROOFING" THE PUDDING

6. TIME-DELAYED REACTIONS

PART THREE: UTILIZING SELF-HYPNOSIS AS A STUDENT

7. IMPROVING YOUR CONCENTRATION, YOUR MEMORY, AND YOUR LEARNING TOOLS

INTRODUCTION

This book contains some of the most efficient methods ever published for acquiring self-hypnosis. The instructions are clear, simple, easy to follow, and ideally graduated. They are grounded on conditioned reflexes solidly anchored in every human being.

It is especially rich in methods of giving oneself posthypnotic suggestions that "work." Some of them are "classics" for the practicing professional hypnotist. They are presented as "proofs-to-myself" of "now-being-in-hypnosis." At the same time, they constitute a step-by-step training toward the use of self-hypnosis—time self-hypnosis, deepening techniques, hand levitation, anesthesia, time distortion, multiple ways of developing a creative visualization—are just a few of them.

I especially liked the three special methods of "eliminating the negative"—the "cloud and the sun," the "burning of the leaves," and the "duck" exercises, called the three basic desensitization techniques.

In the third part, the author discusses the mind power learning methods. Supercharging your willpower, concentration strengthening, memory activation (to the point of a photographic memory), increased speed of reading, maximized retention and recall "on the spur of the need of the moment" are powerfully treated for application to yourself.

Most important in my view are the techniques of creativity in the financial, academic, or artistic field, which the author gives freely to the reader of the book. You will learn how a script writer can actually "prelive" in his mind the next production, audio and video, and then simply "put it down on paper." This technique alone is worth many hundred times the price of the book. The net result is that it constitutes a rich mine of information, and "bread and butter information" for the practicing hypnotist.

Gil Boyne, *Hypnotherapist*
Executive Director,
American Council of Hypnotist Examiners
Glendale, CA 91204

HOW TO GET THE BEST RESULTS
FROM THIS BOOK

Read the whole book once. Then, start
with Part Two: "Acquiring Self-Hypnosis."
Stick to it until you get passing grades as
you go along.

In developing self-hypnotic techniques
to be used as a student (Part Three),
stick to a given goal until you obtain
satisfactory results, then move on to
another goal.

PART ONE

Getting Acquainted with Hypnosis

CHAPTER 1

Self-Hypnosis: A Tool for Success, A Key to Genius

A Natural Gift that Can Be Acquired

Students and scholars of the coming generations may well regard genius with a little less admiration and awe than did their predecessors.

In fact, they will likely be using for themselves the "secret technique that explains it all."

Self-hypnosis, as it can now be inferred from the life history of numerous geniuses of the past, may have been the sporadic, spontaneous, and unexplained phenomenon behind the superior creative abilities of exceptional human beings.

As one pores over the biographies and incidental personal confidences of The Greats, one is constantly made conscious of a common denominator of their lives.

Multiple references are made to a special state of consciousness variously referred to as "trance," "waking dream," "ecstasy," "supra-normal feelings," and so on.

The great poet Tennyson states that when-

3

ever he would, in the quiet of the woods, repeat his own name to himself, over and over again, he would suddenly feel transported into a new state of consciousness in which colors were more vivid and sounds more ethereal, a state in which words came to him, and not only words but phrases and sentences and verses, and that he thereafter had only to copy them onto paper.

At the University of Strasbourg, some of the more notable adherents to the classes in hypnosis were Goethe, Metternich, and Chopin, which demonstrates their interest in the subject, if not their desire to explain to themselves some of the phenomena they were observing in their own psyches.

Some have pretended that Mozart composed the whole of *Cosi fan Tutte* under the so-called spell of hypnosis. It is common knowledge that Mozart would often go for a ride in a coach and, while thus relaxing, hear melodies and orchestrations which he then merely had to write down. Such a spontaneous auditory hallucination can most easily be achieved in a subject trained in self-hypnosis.

According to Kroger (in *Clinical and Experimental Hypnosis*), Rachmaninoff, "who had been unproductive for several years, reportedly composed one of his famous concertos following posthypnotic suggestion."

A Tool for Success

Self-hypnosis may also have been the secret behind a few enormous financial successes. And again it may be inferred to have been the "Aaron's rod" that tapped the fount of creativity used by a great many inventors.

George Washington Carver, "the man who talked with the flowers," specifically says (in Glenn Clark's book bearing the aforementioned title): "All my life, I have risen regularly at four o'clock and have gone into the woods and talked with God. There He gives me my orders for the day . . ."

In the same book, Glenn Clark relates: "Mr. Edison (Thomas) believes that his inventions come through him from the infinite forces in the universe—and never so well as when he is relaxed."

Henry Ford went into "the solitude of his meditating room" to solve problems and prepare his plans of operation.

In the fourteenth chapter of his book *Think and Grow Rich* (titled "The Sixth Sense"), Napoleon Hill talks about his daily hallucinatory "meeting" with nine great men—Emerson, Paine, Edison, Darwin, Lincoln, Burbank, Napoleon, Ford, and Carnegie—his "invisible counselors."

During these meetings, "just before I go to sleep," he acted as chairman for the Executive Board of Himself, which decided upon the action to be undertaken for the realization of his life program. Not wanting to label the experience as self-hypnosis, he takes pains to explain that, "lest I be misunderstood, I wish to state most emphatically that I still regard my cabinet meetings as being purely imaginary . . . while . . . they have led me into glorious paths of adventure . . . encouraged creative endeavor."

Solitude, meditation, relaxation, talking with God or imaginary counselors, how closely—except in name—this resembles hypnosis!

One could thus multiply "ad indefinitum" the

examples taken from history and demonstrate that numerous great figures—artists, writers, painters (refer to the creation of the paintings of the Sistine Chapel as portrayed in the film *The Agony and the Ecstasy*), and inventors have used the "natural gift" of self-hypnosis for the purpose of elevating themselves above the standard levels of achievement.

Yet, the student of these coming years will be able to acquire the same technique by voluntary training.

Of course, it may become a problem to be considered a genius in times when everybody knows how to become a genius.

But what happens in the meantime?

Self-hypnosis will gradually become a choice technique for "getting the edge on competition," on the individual or the collective level.

Some students, some business persons, some of the people engaged in the creative arts and/or professions will have heard about the technique, trained themselves in it, and used it to their own advantage, while the rest of the crowd will keep wondering "how in tarnation" they are doing it.

Of course, before the "Age of Genius" arrives, medical hypnosis will have found a greater number of uses but, at the same time, numerous new applications will also have been devised in the field of nonmedical hypnosis.

In other words, hypnosis will soon be used just as much for "normal" people as it will be used for "abnormal" conditions.

Self-hypnosis, as a matter of fact, is today a much used tool for transforming a normal person into an "above-normal" one.

It is being used as a technique for self-betterment not only for special groups, but for the general public, or at least those members of the general public who have become aware of its existence and its possibilities.

Self-hypnosis is already becoming more commonly used by students and people engaged in creative careers—artistic or professional.

Self-Hypnosis for Students

Concentration

It is a well-known fact that self-hypnosis can be used advantageously by students for the purpose of increasing the efficiency of their memories. Through self-hypnosis, and the posthypnotic suggestions it permits, students can enhance their attention at the moment of intake of information and knowledge—in class or during study; concentration can be sharpened (freedom from interferences and/or mind wandering) while studying, and self-hypnosis can also facilitate the recall of the desired information as needed.

Moreover, through appropriate posthypnotic suggestions, it is possible to improve the integration of the material absorbed into the general pool of knowledge already possessed, together with projecting it into its natural conclusions, thus somehow linking the past and the future through the present.

Studying on the Double

What is much less known about the application of self-hypnosis to the tasks of the student is the fact that he or she can apply an accelerated method of studying which can easily cut by one half—and even two-thirds—the time necessary for the absorption of a given amount of knowledge or double the amount of material absorbed in a given time.

The instrument used for the previously mentioned purpose is time distortion; the author has trained some musicians in a similar "mental" method of practicing their instruments. Such mental practicing consisted in their imagining themselves doing "one hour" of subjective time practicing during five minutes of actual clock time.

That mental practicing had the same automating effect upon their fingers as if they had actually been spending one hour in playing their instrument manually.

Photographic Memory

Another fact, even less well known, is that by systematic training in mental visualization, a student can actually—at the moment of an exam—"copy" the answers unto his paper, word for word, as he "sees" them on the mental screen of his or her brain.

As a matter of fact, self-hypnotic training can be effectively used to create the so-called photographic type of memory.

Sleep Learning

A student who wants to use self-hypnosis "to the hilt" can still augment his or her efficiency as a "learning computer" by using sleeping hours, without the generally vaunted aid of a tape recorder. Posthypnotic suggestions can be used to have the mind take over the "milling" of a given material before the inception of natural sleep.

Self-Hypnosis for the Layperson

Self-Motivation

Of course, students can also avail themselves of those advantages of self-hypnosis that are at the disposal of all other users of self-hypnosis. The first and most important of these "general" advantages of self-hypnosis is self-motivation.

Success Motivation

Through self-hypnosis this can be much more than a periodic "bootstrap operation." Not only can it project on the screen of the mind the enjoyment of a goal that acts as a self-chosen compulsion promoting the ideal daily behavior, but it can also serve to project the gradual step toward achieving such a goal. Self-motivation, by the daily "contemplation" of the objective, can act as the most powerful motivator toward a given achievement, making all deterrents inoperative and side interests unimportant in comparison with the pleasure of the contemplated final result.

Self-hypnosis can also be used to detect the subconscious obstacles to success and to overcome them.

Elimination of Fatigue

Another "automatic" fringe benefit of self-hypnosis, when properly applied and practiced, is the elimination of fatigue. This goal is attained through the self-recharging that is automatically realized by a period of self-hypnotic relaxation and by the systematic elimination of the energy wasters of negative emotions, attitudes, moods, and environmental factors.

Adequate training in self-hypnosis can be used spontaneously and automatically to change any such negative factors through automatic control of emotions.

Self-Hypnosis as a Fount of Creativity

Numerous and quite interesting considerations could here be offered to explain *why* self-hypnosis can be and is a boon to human creativity.

However, it is evidently more interesting for readers to learn *how* it can help them by giving definite examples of its uses by other people.

As to the actual procedures, they are quite simple. Users of self-hypnosis have learned how to initiate hypnosis for themselves, for any predetermined length of time measured in seconds, minutes, or hours, at their own volition. And subjects have been trained to do it anytime, anywhere.

They have also created for themselves, through the assistance of their instructor in self-hypnosis, some mental tools that are required for imagination to function creatively. They have been trained in the use of those tools and have become proficient in their manipulation.

As a matter of course, during their training, they have been rehearsing them by practicing some creative exercises. It then remains for them to perfect through constant use a technique that has been given them during their training.

In other words, their training has been done in two phases: They have learned to produce hypnosis for themselves and then they have learned how to use it.

Hypnosis Is Simply a Condition

In fact, it can never be emphasized enough that, both in medical and in nonmedical hypnosis, the real work begins only *after* the so-called hypnotic sleep has been induced. Too much stress has been placed on the assumption that hypnosis per se is a tool of self-improvement or hereto-improvement.

To repeat: It is only *after* hypnosis has been induced that the real work begins. And therein lies the difference between a hypnotist and a hypnologist, the first being someone trained in "putting people to sleep" and the other having the knowledge of what to do with it once he or she has produced it.

As will be further elaborated in the next chapter, hypnosis is a condition, a mental state in which the conscious mind is bypassed in order to inject blueprints into the subconscious mind. It is a condition—in fact, one of the conditions—and the fastest means of:

1. Injecting suggestions into the subconscious mind.
2. Enhancing the natural capacities of the mind.

Self-hypnosis is a tool and the possession of it does not produce success any more than the mere possession of a scalpel makes one a surgeon.

Self-Hypnosis

With this instrument at their disposal, let us see how some professionals would proceed to use it.

Let it be stated here, once and for all, that the following applications have actually been taught to some people in the professions or occupations indicated.

An architect puts himself "to sleep" for five minutes, after telling his subconscious mind to produce for him, for example, "twelve different treatments of the facade" of a given building which he has to submit to a customer.

After the predetermined time has elapsed (the period of time could just as easily be three or two minutes), he "wakes up"; he has "seen" the twelve different designs of the facade and can now proceed to sketch them on paper.

If none of those sketches pleases him, he can repeat the procedure to get "another dozen sketches," just as easily and quickly as he got the first.

Had he approached the problem in the "normal" manner, he would still have found the twenty-four different frontages of the building, but it would have taken him the "normal" time—not three or five minutes, but three or five days, weeks, or months, according to his normal degree of creativity.

A lawyer, using the same self-hypnosis technique, instantly recalls to memory the source and numbers of some precedents which she *knows* she has read somewhere, and which she now needs to quote in a given case she has before the court.

A lawyer trained in self-hypnosis (one who is reputedly the greatest criminal lawyer in the country) uses a similar technique for finding:

1. How he will present his case in the first place.
2. Which angle is most likely to influence the type of jury he has to deal with.
3. Which witness has told him something differently from which witness at two different points in a long trial.
4. Which witness has subtly contradicted himself in the course of the trial.

One of the best known criminal lawyers of the United States is reported to be a regular user of self-hypnosis.

A scriptwriter, working on a radio or television series, puts himself "to sleep" after asking his subconscious mind to *produce* for him the next episode in his serial production.

During the course of his "sleep" he sees and hears, being produced on the screen of his own mind, the action of his characters just as he would if he were then witnessing a preview of the episode, which in fact he is.

After "coming out of it," all he has to do is to write it down, just as he heard and saw it. Here again, if more verisimilitude or more "life" is required in the episode than has been supplied in the first "preview," all he has to do is to ask for another one.

We know these things may sound fantastic and they are, but they represent actual applications of self-hypnosis to creativity as the author has witnessed them. They are true to facts.

The French writer Honoré de Balzac illustrates, in his two books *Seraphita* and *Louis Lambert*, similar instances of "trance inspirations." Gustave Flaubert and Emile Zola also relate equivalent procedures in their own creativity.

The technique illustrated here for a scriptwriter could evidently be adapted by a novelist, a poet, a fiction or nonfiction writer. This technique is tantamount to a special form of "automatic writing," but it differs from it in the measure that the process is here controlled and consciously provoked.

A painter, wishing to illustrate a given theme, or symbolize a given emotion or idea, can use the same hypnotic type of "inspiration" which has already been described.

In his "mind's eye," he would then, in vivid colors, see two, three, or more realizations of the proposed production. Once more, let us recall the similar methods described in the film *The Agony and the Ecstasy*, by which Michelangelo "imagined" the subject matter illustrating the ceilings of the Sistine Chapel.

A musician, using the very same technique, can get his subconscious mind to produce a new melody, a different arrangement of a given theme, or a full-length concerto or symphony.

With his "mind's ear," he can hear the music, in the selfsame fashion that melodies "just came by themselves" to Mozart as he rode in his coach.

The musician could also use the novel technique of having his subconscious mind "translate into sound" for him the sight of different sceneries, as well as the feeling of different emotions.

A dilettante could use the same techniques for having his subconscious mind translate into images the impressions he gets from the hearing of a piece of music.

A research scientist, still using the same and similar techniques, can accelerate the creative process in herself and use it to find new techniques, new applications of her science, new laws and new theories in pure science.

In this case, the procedure used by the subconscious mind may be the sudden juxtaposition of two ideas which hitherto had never been associated before; it may be the spontaneous detection of a hidden thread in a series of facts already observed by her and leading to the unsuspected discovery of a new theory; it can be the sudden realization of an analogy between parallel situations in two wholly different disciplines; it can be the instantaneous explosion of a long-awaited solution to a problem; it can be the hypnotic dissolution of inhibitions of thought which thus far had prevented her from accepting a novel conclusion.

These were the methods naturally and spontaneously used in the invention of the Fuchsian series by Poincaré, the discovery of cyclic chemistry by Kekule, and the discovery of some of the elements of the atomic bomb by Walter Russel, long before it became a reality.

Much has yet to be investigated and researched about the true process of discovery and creativity; the systematic study of creativity through hypnotic "concentration" might very well become a whole field in itself.

It has already been demonstrated by the studies of Dr. Rhine (on the phenomena of telepathy, at Duke) that hypnosis has been used for creating the proper receptive frame of mind and for eliminating "human and environmental" interferences.

Self-Hypnosis for Businesspersons

To all and sundry, self-hypnosis offers primarily and automatically an ideal mode of relaxation and, when properly applied, constitutes the real secret of how never to be tired.

To businesspersons self-hypnosis provides that same automatic source of relaxation and recuperation, plus many other benefits, few of which are presently known to them.

The problem of finding new products, or new applications or outlets for existing products—currently studied in group brainstorming—can be much better exploited through self-hypnosis; self-hypnosis *is* a one-person brainstorm, offering the advantage that it can be applied to the very person or persons best qualified for producing the desired results, instead of counting on the spontaneous production of many minds rendered free of inhibitions through the very permissive atmosphere of the brainstorming session itself.

What is vastly more important, self-hypnosis can be used by a businessperson to project a personal plan covering the six or twelve coming months, in terms of so much increase in returns, or decrease in expenditures.

To the manager, it can also permit a program to evolve of hitherto unused fields for profit in allied or parallel lines of endeavor.

For instance, a businessperson can ask of his or her subconscious mind: "How can I increase my returns by 50 percent this year?"

and get answers that might otherwise have taken months to learn.

For salespersons, self-hypnosis is above all a tool for success, giving them the motivation necessary to reach a given goal. After all, success is simply a goal, a plan for attaining it and the time and determination needed to reach it, which erodes our perseverance span.

Experience teaches us that it is not so much the goal or the plan that is lacking, but the sometimes long, drawn-out period of perseverance, and the amount of enthusiasm necessary to execute the plan and realize the objectives.

Motivation to success is far from being the sole use of self-hypnosis for salespersons, and those we know do find for it a vastly greater array of applications.

Once trained in mental visualization, they use it for perfecting—by hallucinated "dummy practice"—their prospecting methods, their techniques of handling objections, or their presentation.

Special training in the control of emotions and attitudes can instantly bring them back to that acme of enthusiasm and "go-get-it" which salespeople term "being in top form."

"Top form" is that earnestness and drive by which you can "sell refrigerators to the Eskimos," and be so convinced of the worth of the services you are rendering the prospect by selling him that you "feel sorry for the prospect if he does not buy."

Success motivation is one of the elements of personality on which self-hypnosis can be most efficiently used.

To people engaged in creative activities, to students desirous of surpassing themselves, and to the average person, self-hypnosis presents the real key to success we have read about in hundreds of books on self-help.

It does seem as if, after all is said and done, the true secret more or less diluted in the numerous volumes extolling the "power within," the "inner power," the "power of the mind," the "magic of believing," and all the other techniques, methods, disciplines and/or systems for success is truly self-hypnosis under a disguise.

CHAPTER 2

Objective: Discovering Your Own Electronic Brain

A Blinding Truth

The Eyes Have Never Seen Anything

No matter how surprising such a statement may seem at first "sight," it is nevertheless entirely true and can be understood quite easily.

Each individual is provided with five well-known energy transformers, which have been called the sense organs, or "windows looking unto the world."

The eye is one of your openings on the world, and the general belief that the eyes do see is simply due to the complacent habit of taking things for granted.

The eye is nothing but a living camera. It is equipped with a self-adjusting mechanism that automatically focuses it on an object placed in front of it. It is also naturally conditioned to deal with the intensity of the light impinging on it by varying the opening of its front aperture, called the pupil.

If you place an object facing a pinhole punched in the side of any closed box, the image of that object (in reverse: upside down and right to left) will form itself on the inner wall of this "camera obscura." Such is the principle of the photographic camera.

Similarly, if you place an object in front of your eye, the image of that object will form itself on the inner wall located at the back of the eye, which is called the retina. In the camera, the retina is replaced by an acetate film coated with a thin emulsion of silver chloride in gelatin. Rays of light radiating from the object decompose the silver chloride in various degrees on the area where the image is to appear, proportionately to the intensity of the light reflected onto each point of impact.

The image on a negative is originally a pattern —a reticule—of variously deep chemical changes and is nothing else until it is fixed by the dissolution of the unaffected silver chloride.

In the eye, the photographic plate, the retina, is variously affected in its different points (proportionately to the amount of light impinging upon a given point). The image is a reticule of chemical changes in the cells of the retina (rods and cones), and is nothing else until it is fixed by another operation.

That other operation is the transformation of "chemical" reticule into an electrical one, which is transferred onto the back (occipital part) of the brain.

And, at that moment, you see. *Your brain sees.*

It is thus true that the eyes do not see, that they have never seen and will never see anything. It must therefore be admitted as a possibility that the brain can see without the cooperation of the eyes because it *always* does the seeing in the first place.

The Ears Have Never Heard Anything

The ear is another one of those energy transformers that supplies the brain with the final transformation product of an outside stimulus called sound.

It does not hear; it transforms a given frequency range of vibrations into electrical impulses in the same way a microphone does it, and then feeds the electrical signals to the brain, to an area located on the temporal lobes.

It is therefore equally true that the ear does not hear, that it has never heard anything and never will hear anything.

Incidentally, it is a much more frequent occurrence than is generally imagined that people "hear things" without any "explainable" source of sound to account for the experience. Of course, they very seldom mention the fact, lest they be considered slightly deranged.

Paradoxes Galore

By following a similar reasoning, it can thus be concluded that:

> The eye has never seen anything.
> The ear has never heard anything.
> The nose has never smelled any odor.
> The taste buds have never tasted anything.
> The hand, or the skin, have never touched anything.

The Brain Does It All

As a matter of truth, one must recognize the total dominance of the brain as the real subject of all sensory perceptions.

The brain does the seeing.
The brain does the hearing.
The brain does the smelling.
The brain does the tasting.
The brain does the touching.

Not only does the brain dominate all sensorial functions, but it also dominates the human functions of feeling (through the thalamus, science says today), and thinking, and acting.

Everyone is now aware that the brain controls all the vital functions, such as the beating of the heart, the growth of hair and all the tissues, the digestion of food, assimilation and elimination, and so on.

Corollary

However, the important conclusion to draw here is that: Once a given sensation—an audiogram, a videogram, or any other type of sensogram—has been registered or, better still, printed in the brain, the brain no longer needs the offices of the sense in order to reproduce the corresponding sensogram.

Everyone knows, if only through the evidence of dreams, that one can, without the use of one's eyes, see anything that has already been seen. One can thus hear anything that has already been heard or, generally speaking, feel any sensation that has already been sensed, without the presence of the appropriate outside stimulus.

This is what Yoga calls the separation of the senses and their objects.

The Wilder Penfield Experiments

In the course of his research on cancer of the brain, Wilder Penfield, the universally known brain specialist, had to deal with one of the symptoms of cancer of the brain, a frequently recurring dream that the patient had long before the detection of the brain tumor.

Pursuing his mental deductions, Doctor Penfield performed a trepanation on a patient, probing which involved the exposed brain with a fine electrical needle. After exploring different areas on the cortex, he finally discovered a point which, when electrically stimulated, provoked —in the fully waking state of the subject—the sought after recurrent dream.

He then theorized that the spot that responded to electrical stimulation by provoking the dream must be the one affected by the cancerous growth. He then burned out the suspect microscopic area and stopped the cancerous growth.

During his explorations of the brain, however, when he touched other spots on the brain, the patient would suddenly "see himself," at age six or eight, attending class, and see his classmates and his teacher as if he had actually been attending the class.

This inevitably leads to the conclusion that sensory perceptions are somehow spatially located in the brain and can be restimulated under the proper stimulus, in this case an electrical needle.

These experiments have become one of the outstanding proofs of the well-known observation that nothing is ever forgotten of what one has ever lived, that it is somehow printed in the brain and that it can somehow be re-evoked under certain stimuli.

The perceptions of the senses are somehow written in the brain; they have become sensograms at the very instant they were experienced and, in that very instant, they have become a type of printed circuit.

Further, the whole experiential content of any event one ever lives at any moment is printed in the brain: perceptions, ideations, emotions, actions and all, in the form of what may be called "viveograms."

Printed Circuits Are Constellations

The component parts of those events are printed in different parts of the brain, in the manner of electrical constellations or arborizations, whose components are distributed here and there in the brain, but which can be reintegrated under the proper stimuli.

How You Perceive an Orange

Let us now suppose that you are examining an orange for the first time in your life. The mere act of taking the orange in your hands excites a quantity of minute sense terminals residing just below your skin; some of them are sensitive to touch, others to pressure, others to temperature, and so on.

The electrical signals emitted by those nerves are sent first to your spinal column and from there to your brain—in fact to an area bordering the lateral bulk of the brain. Others will be distributed to different areas to register the dimensions, the shape of the orange, the texture of its rind, and such.

Coming from your eyes, nerve impulses will somehow "organize" different cells of your brain to register the color and other visual aspects of the orange, such as the appearance of the oblong vesicles that you will find when you have peeled it.

Other cells, in other areas of the brain, will register the taste of the orange and, in still other areas of your brain, groups of cells will organize themselves to register the circumstances of the event, such as the temperature of the room, the sunshine coming through the windows onto the orange, and so on.

And all these details are registered in diverse parts of the brain. Thus far, consideration has been given only to the circuits printed on the cortex, the outer zone of your brain.

But that is far from being the whole picture.

In another part of the brain, the thalamus is at the same time registering the emotions that accompany the perception of that orange.

And so, for the simple perception of an orange, a vast electrical network of cerebral cells is appropriately affected to register the event.

Later on, or at that moment, you will associate the word *orange* to that object you now have in your hands. Later, perhaps, the equivalent words in Spanish or Italian or German will again be associated with this entire printed circuit.

And the constellation will continue to grow as you add to your knowledge of oranges; and the entire arborization will later be reactivated by the stimulus of any facsimile of it that will suffice to excite it, oftentimes a single component of the whole constellation, such as the name.

The Role of the Conscious Mind

And what is your conscious mind doing all that time?

It observes, one at a time, the different sensorial impressions that are fed into your subconscious mind—the physical seat of which is the whole nervous system and principally the brain.

It is a witness to the process, just like the operator of an electronic brain who looks at the dials and takes the readings.

It is not the agent that distributes the numerous components of the perception in various parts of the brain. Generally, it does not even suspect their existence.

During that time, the subconscious mind has picked up a whole gamut of additional information that your conscious mind has not noticed, such as the shape, color, and pattern of the drapes in the room, the pieces of furniture about you, and a quantity of such details.

And later, under hypnosis, you could be made to resee the whole thing, one detail at a time, because hypnosis is one of the states of mind in which the conscious mind can become a witness taking inventory of what is in the subconscious mind.

As you are reading these lines, your conscious mind may now "fish back" in your subconscious mind the facts that the orange is something reddish-yellow, sweet, pulpy, and so on.

Circuit Resonance

And so, for each perception, for each sensation, and each event that happens or has happened in your life, an entire constellation of neutral patterns is printed in your brain, a constellation that never seems to erase itself, as shown by the experiments of Wilder Penfield and the various demonstrations of hypnosis.

Such a constellation is subject to the stimulus-response mechanism. It may be restimulated by any element of itself or—better yet—by any reasonable approximation or facsimile of itself.

Henceforth, when someone begins to talk to you of "a reddish-yellow fruit, round, with a slightly pitted rind, sweet to the taste . . .," you will be thinking of an orange.

Similarly, if I now begin to describe to you "a furry quadruped, with a short bushy tail, and long ears, famous for its craving for carrots . . .," you have already thought of a rabbit.

Everything happens as though there were in the brain some associative area, the function of which is to provoke, through an instantaneous type of electrical resonance, the restimulation of all electrical constellations that possess a given common element, when that element acts as a stimulus.

And that common element may be sensorial, ideational, emotional, or motor.

Thus, if I mention the word *yellow*, you can instantly retrace the following constellations:

> Butter
> Orange
> Sun
> Gold

Aunt Alice's dress
and so on

Your "Viveotapes"

For every event in our life, a whole galaxy of constellations is formed to register the sensorial circumstances. The physiological conditions of the moment, the feelings, the surroundings, and the time involved, all are somehow registered in the brain, subconsciously.

Making them much more complete than the videotape, the subconscious mind constantly works at registering the viveotape of our life.

And that viveotape can be replayed in sequence for any "length" of it.

Or a single stimulus can provoke the instantaneous pickup of bits, however widely distributed on the tape, which contains that stimulus as a common element.

This is truly a universe in which the "bat of an eye makes the stars twinkle."

A hypnotic suggestion is a "custom-printed" part of our viveotape made up of desirable "resonators."

Any word, any sentence or gesture, any stimulus can thus be likened to a "fishing hook" lowered into the subconscious mind. Any stimulus is a resonating vibrator that activates, somehow, and to a certain degree, the synchromeshed responses in all the constellations ever registered in the subconscious mind.

More Corollaries

Thinking

What is generally called thinking is merely a continuous unwinding of the myriad of images thus stored in the brain in the form of electronic constellations, each word or each idea or emotion bringing on the next, under the laws of association of ideas.

Such is the basis of Freud's "free association," or "daydreaming aloud," or "thinking aloud."

Memory

That which is called memory is the resonance of the accumulated and related printed circuits under the stimulus of a question coming from the outside or from oneself.

The more vividly the connected printed circuits have been impressed in the neural loci, the richer the constellations that contain the basis of information searched, the easier and the more rapid is the recall.

Imagination

Imagination is the faculty of rearranging into a new image any number of parts of previously acquired constellations.

It functions under the computerlike laws of resonance of the different constellations under the probing of a given "theme."

Conditioned Reflexes

It can readily be seen that, in the case of the perception of an orange, the condition of the integration of the different elements of an orange into a constellation is merely the proximity *in space* of those elements.

In case of conditioned reflexes, it is the proximity *in time* that becomes the condition for constellating two different bits of experience, to use the computer language.

Thanks to the work of Ivan Pavlov, we have a better understanding of the immense role played by conditioned reflexes in daily life, in our methods of thinking, in learning, and in our stimulus-response mechanism.

It is because of his research on conditioned reflexes that we can now better understand the secrets of human learning and of hypnotism.

Hypnotism

Everyone knows the story of Pavlov and his dogs. Every time he would take food to a dog, a bell would be rung, and the secretion of saliva provoked by the meat stimulus would be measured.

After a few hundred repetitions with the meat, the sole sound of the bell would provoke the same amount of salivation.

It was then deduced after experiments were done on a sufficiently large number of subjects, that:

When two or more stimuli happen together, one of which naturally produces a physiological effect, and the other is merely associated in time with it, it happens that, after a certain number of repetitions, the neutral stimulus produces the same effect as the stimulus, which is casually related with the said effect.

Everything happens as if:

Simultaneity equals causality for the brain.

Such a result is not logical, but it is true to fact.

It is unbelievable, but it is true.

It is absurd, but it is quite easily demonstrable.

In the same fashion, a woman "insulted" by an overstimulated lover, in a garden full of roses—with or without the benefit of moonlight—will later develop an allergy to roses.

Learning

It is through a similar process of conditioned reflex that you believe that a piece of furniture that has four legs and a top on which you can either write, eat, or lean is a table.

But try and make a German, or a French person, or a Spaniard, or an Italian believe that such a piece of furniture is a "table" and listen to his or her vehement protestations.

To them, that is not a table, but *ein Tisch, une table, una mesa,* or *una tavola,* respectively.

They merely have been conditioned differently than you have; associated the object with a different sound, a different bell.

Hypnotism Defined

Hypnotism is the quickest method known by which an operator does somehow:

1. Bypass the conscious mind.
2. Restimulate a facsimile of natural sleep.
3. a. exploit the printed circuits of the subconscious mind or
   b. print new desirable circuits or erase old, undesirable ones through suggestion or reflex conditioning, or
   c. accelerate or ameliorate the natural mental processes.

In other words, hypnotism is a choice technique for exploiting the subconscious, by bypassing the conscious mind.

In *hetero-hypnosis*, the operator is another human.

In *self-hypnosis*, the operator is your own conscious mind.

Trademarks of the Conscious and Subconscious Minds

The subconscious mind works automatically; totally lacks the capacity of evaluation; has no awareness of its own processes; cannot perform any criticism or examination of what goes into it; it is the full storehouse, at one and the same time, of all previous acquisitions; and never sleeps.

The conscious mind has the power of choice; has awareness of what goes on—one thing at a time—in the subconscious mind or the environment; can evaluate—by referral to the inner computer of the subconscious mind; has the faculty of criticizing before it accepts; can hold only one idea at a time in its focus; has the power of will; and can go to sleep or be awake.

Let us remember: It is not the subconscious mind that goes to sleep: it cannot do it while you are alive.

Dangers of Hypnosis

Because it is only *one* of the methods of exploiting the powers of the subconscious mind, hypnosis is no more dangerous than any of the other methods and techniques of doing it.

It all depends on the operator.

Various Methods of Bypassing the Conscious Mind

In the definition of hypnosis, we have stated that it is *one*—and the quickest—method known to bypass the conscious mind. It is far from being the only one or the most subtle method. Hypnosis offers this advantage over the other methods: You can recognize it readily by the fact that its setting, by definition, comprises the *facsimile* of natural sleep.

Other techniques exist for bypassing the conscious mind and exploiting the subconscious

mind—for the advantage of the operator much
more than the advantage of the subject.

Some of the more obvious ones could thus be
stated:

> **HABITS**—They *are* automatic.
>
> **INDOCTRINATION**—Think of Hitler.
>
> **REPETITION**—The "most eloquent fig-
> ure of speech," said Napoleon: the fa-
> vorite method of "big" advertising.
>
> **MONOIDEISM**—A technique used in
> quite a few mental disciplines.

In the definition of hypnosis that we have
proposed, note the word *somehow.* ("Somehow
bypass the conscious mind.")

The somehows are indeed quite numerous. A
short list would compromise the following:

> Conditioned reflexes
> Trickery
> Drugs
> Rhythm, such as dance
> Fear
> Faith
> Authority
> Prestige
> Relaxation
> Natural sleep
> Persuasion
> Intense emotions, such as anger
> Hyperventilation
> Hypoventilation
> Asceticism
> Concentration
> and others

The Method of This Book

In order to educate you in the proficient use
of self-hypnosis, we will be using, as methods

of bypassing the conscious mind in order to exploit the potentialities of your subconscious mind, the following artifices:

Monoideism
Conditioned reflexes
Repetition

Self-Hypnosis: A Two-Phase Process

Phase 1. You will learn how to—and you will—produce hypnosis in yourself, for a predetermined number of minutes, anytime, anywhere, at will.

Phase 2. You will be tutored in exploiting your own subconscious mind, by using such techniques as will best suit your custom-made needs as a student.

The general approach to those two phases can be seen by consulting the Contents.

PART TWO

Acquiring Self-Hypnosis

CHAPTER 3

Objective: Acquiring Self-Hypnosis

A Bird's-eye View of the Chapter

This chapter is intended to help you acquire four conditioned reflexes.

Those four conditioned reflexes will produce for you:

1. Instantaneous relaxation of the arms.
2. Instantaneous relaxation of the legs.
3. Instantaneous and automatic closure of the eyes.
4. Instantaneous integration of the three previous exercises into one single formula. This formula will thereafter be your key for self-hypnosis.

Note: *At different intervals, you will be cautioned* not *to pass on* to the next exercise *before* you have completed and automatized the previous conditioned reflex.

Therefore, no more time will be spent on the precautionary notice except to explain here, once and for all, that the *gradual* acquisition of self-hypnosis is much easier and faster *if* you follow the practice of acquiring each of the four automatisms explained and described in this chapter, *one at a time*—that is, *successively*.

Dehypnotizing Yourself on Hypnosis

Hypnotists constantly hear a subject contend that he or she "was not under hypnosis because . . ."

To eliminate at the outset some of those sometimes irritating "becauses," let us answer some of the questions that should be answered in order to clarify the experience. Let us now discuss the most usual questions in the order of priority by frequency:

Will I Lose Consciousness?

No matter how deep you go under hypnosis, you will *never* lose consciousness. People who have ever "awakened" during the night to go to the bathroom and claimed the next morning that they "did not remember doing it" have (a) passed from sleep into hypnosis and (b) had themselves a slight case of amnesia without ever taking notice of it.

The experience of "waking up" in the morning, knowing that you were dreaming, turning over in your bed and going back to sleep is another instance of "natural" hypnosis.

Daydreaming could be a fair analogy to hypnosis. Hypnosis is actually a facsimile of a natural sleep "in which you could witness your own sleep"; subjects have even been known to remark that "I heard myself snoring."

So, do not expect to lose consciousness, to go "out of this world," or to experience some extraordinary bit of sensorial or emotional, bizarre condition.

When the stage hypnotist suggests to his subject of the moment that "he is out in the Tropics, that it is 100 degrees and . . . ," the subject, who everyone believes to be "asleep," begins to perspire and proceeds to take off his coat. He must have "heard" the suggestion and, therefore, was not asleep. He was hypnotized, but not asleep.

We repeat: Hypnosis is a state of consciousness in which the conscious mind is somehow bypassed and which elicits a facsimile of natural sleep, but the conscious mind still remains as a witness to the whole affair.

So, do not expect to be asleep, when and as you go under hypnosis. Expect to be in a state of total relaxation, reproducing most of the outer aspects of natural sleep; you will not be asleep.

How Do I Know I Will Awaken?

Contrary to the first group of people, who insist upon losing consciousness, this brand of questioner wants to be reassured that he or she will "come out of it." Not only are these people afraid that they will "go out of this world," they even fear that they may never come back to it.

As all the textbooks on hypnosis will tell you, in hetero-hypnosis, if the operator should happen to drop dead, while he has a subject "under," because the "rapport" is broken two things may happen:

1. The subject will wake up by himself
   or
2. The hypnotic "sleep" will be changed into a state of natural sleep, which would then last, according to the sleep needs of the subject, anywhere from five minutes to a few hours.

Moreover, the exercises you will be practicing in the following pages will permit you to fractionate the effects. The exercises in this chapter will only produce a light hypnoidal state, and you will, before you reach the fifth exercise, have become conditioned to bringing yourself out of whatever hypnosis you may attain, at your own discretion.

Finally, if you should still be fearful of not waking up, just set an alarm clock to five minutes after the beginning of your exercises, and that will be that.

Why Did My Mind Keep Wandering?

If ever hypnotists are called upon to make a list of their pet peeves, this would certainly come as the third item in the series of complaints they would express on their subjects.

In hypnosis, your mind most likely will be wandering because it is natural for the mind to wander, such wandering being merely the subvocal association of ideas, which is commonly called thinking.

We will be using a certain manner of "playing broken record," which will reduce your mind wandering to a minimum, but do not expect that your mind will be so "glued" to the idea you are holding on to—through your "playing broken record"—that it won't wander at all.

So, if you find that your mind does wander during your exercises, just let it wander.

Maybe I Was Trying Too Hard?

The answer to that question has already been given a couple thousand years ago: "Who, amongst you, can increase his stature one inch by his will?"

No amount of willing, of trying, of striving, of helping yourself toward obtaining the goal of each exercise will ever help you one iota.

In fact, the more you try, the less you will succeed.

One should be cautioned about trying to "concentrate." Concentration has, alas, been misleadingly associated with the cramped tension of Rodin's *The Thinker.* The type of concentration you will be called upon to do will be a passive concentration.

The only "trying" that is expected of you is to try and keep your exercises regular.

If you want to demonstrate to yourself the futility of trying to will an effect, if you want to settle the question for yourself once and for all, the following "pencil experiment" will do it for you.

Hold a pencil between your right thumb and index finger. Hold the pencil tight, and now repeat to yourself, mentally: "I *want* to drop this pencil."

You could repeat that affirmation till doomsday and still be unable to drop that pencil. In order to drop it, you must first change your thought to "I am dropping this pencil."

Is It Dangerous?

Hypnosis, being a facsimile of natural sleep, is no more dangerous than natural sleep, or daydreaming. Let us recall once more that a violent burst of emotion, such as anger, makes you just as susceptible to suggestion as hypnosis. Spontaneous productions or projections would no more be provoked by hypnosis than they are by other events in the user's daily life.

How Do I Know I Can Do It Myself?

You can settle this question by a very simple experiment you can make now.

Stand up by a wall, at an approximate distance of ten inches, with your back to the wall, heels together on the floor, eyes closed.

Now, repeat silently: "I am falling to the wall," like a broken record; if you hold that thought in your mind, by merely repeating it like a broken record, you will fall to the wall and convince yourself of the power of *Monoideism*.

You will have demonstrated for yourself the so-called power of the mind. You will know that "any thought that you hold in your mind (or that somebody else hammers into it) long enough will express itself in your body, if it concerns your body, or becomes truth to you."

If you repeat the preceeding sentence, in the manner indicated, and you do *not* fall to the wall, you are still responding to another thought that you had in your mind *before* the exercise or that your own subconscious mind is machine-gunning at the same time as you repeat it.

However, if you let go of the Johny-contrary in you, you will fall to the wall, and that is inevitable.

Acquiring self-hypnosis is merely a sequence of such resonances of the printed circuits in your electronic brain and, having exploited one set, you know you can control the others.

Playing Broken Record

One of the formulas for bypassing the conscious mind in order to exploit the subconscious mind, and producing a facsimile of natural sleep (hypnotizing), is a reduction of the afferent stimuli.

Because each object that your eyes focus upon initiates a train of thoughts, it is immediately evident that you must do those exercises with your eyes closed.

Once more, for the identical reason of reducing the stimulation by the environment, the sentences that you will use will be repeated *mentally*.

Of course, you may be unable to prevent the movements of your lips as you repeat those sentences mentally, mechanically, like a broken record. Subvocalization should not bother you in the least. It should not even be considered as an obstacle.

Obviously, what we mean by "playing broken record" is repeating something in the fashion of a broken record, over and over again, just like a broken record in which the needle constantly returns to the previous groove.

For instance, the first sentence of your first exercise is "My right arm is heavy." After assuming your preferred position, and closing your eyes, you will repeat *mentally* the sentence: "My right arm is heavy" in a continuous, mechanical, machinelike fashion, just as a broken record would do.

Each sentence composing that exercise Number 1 will be repeated approximately ten times. You should not be concerned about the number of times that you have repeated each sentence and whether it was eight, nine, ten, or eleven.

If you find yourself preoccupied with this detail, use the following strategy.

> One—My right arm is heavy.
> Two—My right arm is heavy.
> Three—My right arm is heavy, and so on, up to ten, after which you continue to the next sentence, proceeding in the same fashion.

How to Terminate Each Exercise

Each exercise in this chapter (and in several of the chapters that follow) will automatically be terminated, and without exception, by repeating *three times* the sentence: "Everything is normal."

After each such termination of one exercise, you should get up, stretch, and walk around for about one minute. Then you are ready to repeat the exercise.

This method of terminating each exercise has these aims:

1. Eliminate the residual effects of the previous one.
2. Assure yourself that, when you repeat the exercise, you are not benefiting at the start from the momentum of the preceding exercise.

Body Postures

Two positions are herein described and illustrated for the daily practicing of your exercises. They are the body positions from which you will get the best results because they reduce to a minimum the level of afferent stimuli.

Those exercises should preferably be practiced in a quiet room, under a subdued light, in order to minimize the possibilities of disturbances.

All tight pieces of clothing, all hindrances to the free relaxation of the body (glasses, belt, girdle, tie, wristwatch, etc.) should be loosened or put aside.

Whether you prefer a horizontal or a seated position, some optimal conditions are desirable, even if you should not make a ritual of it.

Lying on a Couch

The student will soon notice whether the lying position (couch or bed) is preferable for him or her. If the prone position is chosen, lie on your back, with the legs slightly parted and relaxed, so that the feet frequently form an open V; a light support under the back of the knees, such as folded bedclothes or a cushion, will help obtain the maximal relaxation of the legs.

Heels should not touch. You can discover the most comfortable positions of the head and the shoulders by trying various methods of supporting them.

The arms are stretched out alongside the body, loose and relaxed. The fingers are slightly parted and preferably should not touch the body.

Sitting Down

The exercises could just as easily be done in a sitting position, on the sole condition of noting certain physiological and anatomical factors.

Choose a chair with a reclining back or a straight-back chair, according to your personal preference.

The back of the reclining chair should be high enough to support the head as it rests comfortably on it. The hands and the fingers should be placed on the arms of the chair; or better yet, hung loosely from the sides of the chair.

The legs should be approximately parallel while the thighs make a slight angle.

The ordinary sitting chair is often the type of seat used because it permits one to practice at any time of the day and in any place.

The feet will be placed squarely on the floor, the hands and arms resting on the lap, the edge of the seat must not apply undue pressure on the thighs or back of the knees.

Use the position in which you would take a nap.

The Price Must Be Right

This book will permit you to acquire self-hypnosis and all its ensuing benefits if you follow the recommendations given.

There is no amount of reading and re-reading you may do that will dispense you in any fashion from actually doing the prescribed exercises —and *passing* them.

In order to acquire anything, and especially a new psychological facility, the right price must be paid.

The price in this case is the conscientious and regular practicing of the exercises. In order to dispose of the natural inertia, it might be a good idea to read the first chapter over and over again, but it is useless to think of passing on to Chapter 4 without first *passing* this third chapter.

Another method of overcoming inertia is to put aside each day a regular time in which to do these exercises. If you spend two sessions per day—two sessions of fifteen minutes each —on the exercises of this chapter, as indicated, and under normal conditions, you should attain a reasonable degree of self-hypnosis within ten to fifteen days.

Some of you may even be able to pass this chapter and get the desired effects within one week.

The speed depends upon your own individuality, but the results can be attained by all with time and practice.

You will find a ton of motivation in the following consideration:

If you have to spend thirty hours of your time, in all, to securing the advantages offered by Chapters 3, 4, and 5 of this book, it is equivalent to gaining five hundred free hours during your college years.

And the advantages of self-hypnosis can be yours for a lifetime.

Exercise Number 1

Aim

Immediate relaxation of arms and neighboring muscles by using five repetitions of one sentence; that sentence is: "Both my arms are heavy as lead."

Method

Mechanical repetition of five different sentences, ten times each—with eyes closed—and of one terminal sentence, three times; that sentence is: "Everything is normal."

Automatic Effects

A gradual acceleration, facilitation, and enhancing of the effects so that the total effect can be obtained by the single repetition of one sentence, five times; that sentence is: "Both my arms are heavy as lead," followed by the same terminal sentence given previously.

Printed circuits used

1. Heaviness of the arms, experienced thousands of times in natural sleep, after a hard day's work or a long, tiresome drive at the wheel of your car.
2. Imagining your muscles as employees going on a strike, as loose and limp as wet rags.

Techniques Used for Bypassing the Conscious Mind

1. Conditioned reflex.
2. Memory bank of the subconscious mind.
3. Repetition.
4. Motivation through desire of goals.

The Broken Record

The five sentences used in succession are:

1. My right arm is heavy.
2. My right arm is very heavy.
3. My left arm is heavy.
4. My left arm is very heavy.
5. Both my arms are heavy as lead.

While the subject repeats these sentences, he passively keeps thinking about his arm, from the tips of the fingers to the very shoulder.

He imagines those muscles to be his employees, which can only do one of two things: either be taut and tense or working, or loose and limp, and not working, going on a strike, as if they got the zero message from headquarters, as wet pieces of string, as elastics he has let go of.

Such imagining has to be done in a passive, relaxed manner.

Procedure

1. Set yourself in the body position of your choice.
2. Close your eyes.
3. Mentally repeat each sentence ten times.
4. Get up, stretch yourself, walk around, and do it once more in the same fashion and then, once more.

Series of Three Per Session

Exercise Number 1 lasts approximately three minutes. Do it three times per session. Each repetition of the exercise is separated by approximately one minute.

Total Duration:

Eleven minutes and that session is over. Ideally, you should do three sessions per day.

Important Notice

Do not divert your attention by trying to be at the same time the actor and the audience, by trying to notice the effects *during* your exercises. You will have ample time to recapitulate the events after your session is over.

Passing Grades

When you can feel the total and immediate relaxation and heaviness of the arms by merely repeating, as indicated in "Aim," five times, the single sentence: "Both my arms are heavy as lead" and then terminating the effect by the three-time repetition of the sentence "Everything is normal," you may pass on to the next exercise, to exercise number two.

Exercise Number 2

Aim

Immediate relaxation of legs and neighboring muscles by using five repetitions of one sentence; that sentence is: "Both my legs are heavy as lead."

The method, the automatic effects, the printed circuits used, the procedure, the series of three exercises per session, the Important Notice already mentioned are the same as those in the Exercise Number 1.

The technique and the broken record method are also the same. The five sentences are even the same *except* in each sentence:

The word *arm* has been replaced by the word *leg*.

The imagined pictures should be the same, and the following sentences are reiterated for the purpose of reinforcement.

They are:

1. My right leg is heavy.
2. My right leg is very heavy.

3. My left leg is heavy.
4. My left leg is very heavy.
5. Both my legs are heavy as lead.

As in the previous exercise, begin by sitting in the accustomed position, closing your eyes, and repeating each sentence ten times (don't worry about the number of times), and terminate the exercise by using the same sentence three times (Everything is normal).

The exercise is again practiced in ten to fifteen-minute sessions permitting three repetitions of the exercise. As in the previous case, don't bother to observe the effects during the exercises, and the same processes of acceleration and facilitation will be observed until you can pass the test.

Passing Exercise Number Two

You can consider yourself as having obtained passing grades when you can feel the total and immediate relaxation and heaviness of the two legs by merely repeating, as indicated in "Aim" for this exercise, five times, the single sentence: "Both my legs are heavy as lead," and then terminating the effect by repeating three times the sentence "Everything is normal."

Exercise Number 3

Aim

Immediate and automatic closure of the eyes by using the given series of five sentences, saying each sentence once.

Method

Mechanical repetition of five sentences, ten times each, the eyes being open at the start, and one terminal sentence, three times; that sentence is: "Everything is normal."

Automatic Effects

The same gradual acceleration of the process as in the previous exercises, so that the total effect can be obtained by the repetition of each sentence once.

Printed Circuits Used

Imagine two tiny but strong magnets glued to the lower and upper lids of each eye and of opposite poles, pulling one another.

The Broken Record

The five sentences used in succession, and each being repeated ten times are:

1. My eyelids are heavy.
2. My eyelids are very heavy.
3. My eyelids are heavy as lead.
4. My eyes are closing.
5. My eyes are closed tight.

Procedure

1. Set yourself in your customary position.
2. Mentally repeat each sentence ten times, as you keep "imagining" the magnets at work.

3. Close your eyes (if you have imagined the magnets they cannot fail
   to close).
4. Repeat the terminal sentence three
   times.
5. Get up, stretch, walk around, and
   repeat to a total of three exercises.

Passing Grades

When your eyes close automatically as you
mentally say each sentence, once to yourself,
you have passed this exercise and you may go
on to the next one.

Exercise Number 4

Aim

Light hypnosis at the count of twenty.

Printed Circuits Used

1. Previous exercises.
2. Association (natural) of eye closure
   with sleep, thereby initiating facsimile of it.
3. Conditioned reflex produced by this
   exercise.

Sentences Used

For this last exercise of this chapter, the student will count each sentence as he repeats it.

The student, having assumed the customary posture, will mentally repeat:

One—Both my arms are heavy as lead.
Two—Both my arms are heavy as lead.
Three—Both my arms are heavy as lead.
Four—Both my arms are heavy as lead.
Five—Both my arms are heavy as lead.

The counts from *six to ten* will be followed by the sentence: Both my legs are heavy as lead.

The counts from *eleven to fifteen* will be followed by the sentences already used when passing the previous exercises, and the counts *sixteen to twenty* will be followed by the sentence: Heavier with each breath, which he will mentally repeat as the condensation of the longer sentence: "My whole body is heavier with each breath." The terminal sentence, as in all previous exercises, will again be: "Everything is normal," repeated three times.

Procedure

It will be sufficient to practice this exercise twice per session.

The use of an alarm clock could, in certain cases, be useful to condition yourself from drifting into natural sleep.

The alarm clock should be set for five minutes, so as to condition the subconscious mind to the time lapse of five minutes for future uses.

Passing Grades

The student may consider that he has passed this exercise when he can get the same effects by the mere counting from one to twenty and then, go on to the next chapter.

General Considerations

As any one of the exercises given in this chapter is practiced by the student, he or she will notice a gradual and steady process of acceleration, facilitation, and intensification of the effects described by the sentences used. The printing and reprinting of the neural patterns increases the "conductivity" of the neural paths concerned, which is another way of saying that practice makes perfect.

Marginal Effects

There sometimes occurs, and there may occur in your case, during the practice of those exercises, some more or less well-defined "fringe effects."

They may be benefits in that they are pleasant and they may be deficits because they are slightly annoying. Those side effects could be sensations of cold, warmth, or itchiness, or automatic motions of the extremities (fingers, for instance).

Some people may have a slight feeling of lightness or dizziness or a slight numbness of one hand, and so on.

As long as those effects are not unpleasant, they might as well be ignored because they will gradually disappear. As you know now, they are due to physiological association with some element of the situation.

If, in some extraordinary case, such sensations should become too disagreeable, consult a certified hypnotist/hypnotherapist. (See page 171.)

CHAPTER 4

Objective: Deepening and Timing Hypnosis

This chapter has two objectives, both of which will be pursued simultaneously: the deepening of the state of slight hypnosis obtained through the previous chapter and the timing of the hypnotic "sleep."

The deepening of the hypnotic state will be effectuated by the use of mental imagery.

The timing will be done by using an alarm clock to "prime" the inner clock, the mechanism that evaluates time, the subconscious mind.

The two phases of this chapter will therefore overlap and the student, should, quite easily, distinguish the alternation of the two objectives as we proceed.

Posthypnotic Suggestions

This chapter introduces the method by which all posthypnotic suggestions are to be given to the subconscious mind; and that method is to make the image—the *blueprint* of the suggestion —before one goes under hypnosis.

The Subconscious Mind

The subconscious mind can be compared to a vast electronic brain or computer. It has been stated that the subconscious mind is the most elaborate, the most perfect, and the most complicated electronic brain that has ever existed.

There is not enough money or enough knowledge to make an electronic calculator that could compare with the subconscious mind. In fact, no one has been able to determine what it cannot do.

It has cured people of diseases cataloged as incurable by medicine, in shrines throughout the world such as Lourdes, Guadeloupe, Ste. Anne de Beaupre, and elsewhere.

It has already been documented in the literature on the subject of the subconscious mind that:

1. It has been known to extract the square or cubic root of any number at the mere suggestion of the problem.
2. It has been known to multiply a six-figure by a ten-figure number instantaneously.
3. Some individuals are able to tell, without any kind of "thinking," the day of the week of any date in history.
4. Edgar Cayce could, without ever having seen the subject, determine which organ or function in his or her body was "out of kilter" and also prescribe, from a number of the ther-

apeutic disciplines, which medicine,
treatment, or adjustment would ef-
fectuate the cure.

And so on.

We know that the subconscious mind is the
reservoir of all perceptions ever amassed up to
this day in your life, and that includes all the
lectures you have ever attended, all the classes
you ever took and all the reading you ever did
in your life.

You could spend an entire lifetime investigat-
ing the potentialities of your subconscious mind
and still not exhaust them. This presentation of
a few of the known facts about the subconscious
mind has been brief, so that you may realize that
such applications as you will be working on
represent only a small fraction of its possibilities.

Similarly, the doubts will be eradicated from
your conscious mind about your capability of
performing these exercises.

Phase One: Training in Deepening Hypnosis

Procedure

Clock-timed hypnosis (for five minutes) plus
visual imagery

Each exercise will be numbered and no standards of visualization should be deemed essential.

Imagery to Be Used

In Exercise Number 5: staircase, escalator,
and elevator.

In Exercise Number 6: a pendulum.
In Exercise Number 7: a hammock.
In Exercise Number 8: slides.
In Exercise Number 9: preferred image.

Note: *In all the exercises of this chapter, no effort should be made to mentally "see" the images suggested.*

Exercise Number 5

You are to put yourself to "sleep" for five minutes.

Before you put yourself to sleep, you make the blueprint that you are going to imagine during those five minutes, without trying, striving, willing, or forcing the effect, as follows:

You are walking down a very long staircase, with heavily carpeted steps so as to absorb the sounds. Each step bears the inscription SLEEP.

On the walls of that staircase at certain intervals you see signs saying SLEEP, or maybe an arrow, pointing toward the bottom of the stairs, saying, DEEP SLEEP, indicating that, as you are walking down that staircase, you are walking into relaxation, into heaviness, into well-being, and toward that identical feeling you might have felt, if you could have, during that night when you slept soundest and deepest, awakened "without waking up," just to witness your own sleep.

At some point on that staircase, you could imagine that you are approaching a landing

where there is an escalator, just as in large
department stores, each step bearing the inscription SLEEP. You then imagine yourself going
down, down, deeper and deeper into that which
has been called hypnotic sleep, but is merely a
facsimile of natural sleep, reproducing the outer
aspects of natural sleep but in which you always remain aware of the outside world, even if
it does seem remote and uninteresting. When
you get off the escalator, you imagine that you
use the staircase again, or that you are now on
a landing, in front of open doors of an elevator,
and then you yourself press the button that
sends the elevator down, at your own good speed,
down, down, deeper and deeper and deeper into
hypnosis. And, when the elevator stops, you
use the staircase or the escalator or the elevator, until the five minutes have elapsed or the
alarm clock rings the five minutes, or you think
to yourself: "Everything is normal," or, count to
yourself, mentally, downward, from 20 to zero.

And this exercise is terminated.

Exercise Number 6

You are to put yourself under, by counting
from 1 to 20, for five minutes.

Before you put yourself to sleep, you make
the blueprint that you are going to imagine,
during those five minutes, without trying, striving, willing, or forcing the effect, the following:

You are observing a pendulum, beating to
and fro, the pendulum beat to the right
meaning *deep* and the pendulum beat to
the left meaning *sleep*.

The pendulum could be a simple bob hanging from a string, or it could be the pendulum of a clock, or it could be the pendulum of a metronome. It could be a Foucault pendulum.

You may vary the speed of the pendulum, making it slower and making it faster, so as to choose that rhythm the subconscious mind prefers; and being the speed the subconscious mind prefers, it will be most effective.

You will keep on imagining that pendulum for the duration of the five minutes, timing yourself with an alarm clock or depending on your inner clock if it has already been adequately trained in that respect.

Note: *Do not worry at this point whether you can "see" with your mind's eye the images suggested. Some of you will not, at this stage of your training; but the mere imagining, whether the mental images be hazy, cloudy, grossly delineated, or totally nonexistent, will produce the intended effect, which is to deepen the hypnosis.*

Later on, exercises will be specifically designed to cultivate the inner vision.

Exercise Number 7

You are to put yourself under for five minutes, with the usual key of counting from 1 to 20.

Before putting yourself to sleep, make the blueprint that you are going to imagine, during those five minutes and without trying, striving, willing to forcing the effect, the following:

You are now lying in a hammock, out in the country somewhere or in your own back-yard. There is beautiful sunshine, the temperature is ideal, and the hammock is stretched between two trees. The branches of the trees protect you from the direct rays of the sun, but permit you to see and watch fleecy white clouds slowly drifting by in the blue sky, just drifting away and taking with them all cares, all worries, all tensions, mental or muscular, and maybe sometimes forming themselves into the semblance of the word *sleep* and then drifting away, only to be replaced by new downy white clouds.

It feels so good to be, in imagination, in that hammock that you feel yourself drifting into sleep (facsimile of natural sleep) and you can almost feel the sway of the hammock and *that* sway of the hammock makes you sleep even deeper until the five minutes has elapsed.

Exercise Number 8

You are to put yourself to sleep for five minutes, observing the conditions already given before the "blueprints" of Exercises 6 and 7, and you imagine the following:

You are now playing that game which we all played when we were young, the game of going down slides.

The slides all terminate onto a mat that says *sleep*, and there are long slides, short slides, slow slides and swift slides, straight slides and some that have a slight curve to them, and you never have to take a ladder to the next slide because there is always one ready to receive you when you have left the previous one, until the five minutes have been timed off by your alarm clock.

Exercise Number 9

You are to put yourself to sleep for five minutes, observing the conditions already outlined, and imagine the following:

You are standing in front of a blackboard; on the blackboard, you draw a circle and, over the circle, in block letters, the word *sleep.*

In the circle you draw a letter A, filling most of the circle, and then you erase the letter A, taking care not to touch the circle. Then, you draw the letter B inside the circle, you erase it in its turn, again taking care not to erase the circle, and then you pass on to letter C, and then letter D and, in the same fashion, all the way down to letter Z and back to A, until the five minutes have been timed by the alarm clock.

Exercise Number 10

Once you have done each of the exercises of this chapter in its turn, you will naturally have found one of those exercises that appeals most to you—that is, to your subconscious mind.

Exercise Number 10 consists in visualizing, for five minutes, that one image chosen among the previous ones of this chapter that the subconscious mind prefers, as determined by your conscious evaluation.

Exercise Number 10 then consists in visualizing the "preferred image" for five minutes, still timing yourself with the alarm clock.

And the practicing of Exercise 10 terminates the first phase of this chapter.

Phase Two: Building an Inner Clock to Time Your Hypnosis

Each of the following exercises in this chapter has the objective of training the inner sense of time to the point where, after a predetermined number of minutes, your eyes just pop open, or you get the urge to open them.

That objective is obtained by a series of exercises using the preferred image and the alarm clock to condition the time sense of your subconscious mind.

Remembering that the machine that makes time for you is the subconscious mind and, recalling the principles of reflex conditioning, you will readily appreciate the way the goal is attained.

The following exercises can therefore be explained quite succinctly.

Exercise Number 11

Five minutes of preferred image, timed with
   alarm clock.
and then,
Four minutes of preferred image, timed with
   alarm clock.
and then,
Three minutes of preferred image, timed with
   alarm clock,
and then,
Two minutes of preferred image, timed with
   alarm clock,
and then,
One minute of preferred image, timed by alarm
   clock.
Quite obviously, this exercise will last approximately fifteen minutes

Exercise Number 12

Exercise Number 12 is the same as Exercise
Number 11.
   But—without the alarm clock.

Note: *No undue concern should be provoked by the inability to subconsciously
time your sleep "to the second," as long*

as you do get the relaxation, the heaviness of the limbs, and the feeling of its "deepening" under the stimulus of visual imagery.

You may have to use your alarm clock for a while, but rest assured that, eventually, you will be able to dispense with it.

At the beginning, your timing may be slightly off, but that will also adjust itself as you proceed.

Exercise Number 13: Deepening and Accelerating the Hypnosis

This exercise consists of putting yourself under for various lengths of time, measured in minutes or seconds. *Always think to yourself before you count to twenty*: "Now, I will sleep for X minutes," and then count from 1 to 20.

While you practice this exercise, you will be using the following suggestion: each time faster and deeper.

Meaning, of course, that every time you put yourself to sleep, your eyes close faster and you go deeper asleep. Now, that suggestion each time faster and deeper.

Either you will be writing it on a blackboard, in your imagination,

> or it will be written on a blackboard,
>> or the writing of it will be done on a piece of paper,

or it will be in the form of a neon sign, flashing on and off or "staying put,"

or it will be written in the sky by an airplane,

or it will repeat itself mentally like a broken record,

or you may even *hear* it being repeated to you,

or it may be projected in any other fashion that your subconscious mind or your conscious mind prefers.

This exercise will be practiced for various periods of time, measured in minutes or seconds, as you already know how to do.

The importance of practicing the self-induction for 10, 15, or 20 *seconds* will come to be appreciated later in the course of the book.

CHAPTER 5

Objective: Entertaining Yourself and "Proofing" the Pudding

Aim of This Chapter

The aim of this chapter is multifold. The experience gained in teaching self-hypnosis over the last two decades has taught us that no amount of advice that the time spent in "proving to myself that I really go under" might better be used for further training in the techniques of self-hypnosis is persuasive. Students still want to secure "the proof."

So, the first aim of this chapter is to quench that inevitable thirst.

However, the tests provided here will also serve to train the student in the control of the subconscious processes of his or her mind. After all, self-hypnosis is simply the art of training the subconscious in the consciously provoked elicitation of its potentialities.

Moreover, the exercises suggested will, by their very entertaining nature, both eliminate some of the hard-work aspects of this practical course and foster the motivation to keep on practicing.

Exercise Number 14

Note: *We will begin with in-hypnosis suggestions, that is, suggestions that will be carried out by the subconscious mind during the hypnotic period.*

At this point, the degree of success in those tests will vary both in speed and in completeness with each subject.

Keep in mind that the effects will be subject to the same laws of facilitation and acceleration frequently mentioned so far.

Serious students should be content with *one* of the present tests and pass on to the real practice of developing such subconscious skills as are valuable in studying; those are found in the following chapters.

The in-hypnosis suggestion will be:

> The levitation of one arm, that arm being the most muscularly developed arm—the right arm for right-handed people and the left one for the left-handed student.

Procedure

You will:

1. First make the blueprint of what you want to happen during the hypnosis,
2. Then, go to sleep for five minutes,
3. Let the subconscious (George) do the job.

Blueprint

As you go to sleep, you will imagine that there is a fairly large balloon tied to your right wrist. The balloon is filled with helium gas and therefore provides a strong antigravity, upward-pulling force. You will first feel a lessening of the pressure of your right hand on whatever support it is then leaning upon (your lap, your thigh, or the arm of the chair or the couch), then, a sensation of floating in your whole right hand, the sensation your right hand would have *if* it were immersed in a liquid where it loses the equivalent in weight of the liquid displaced, and your fingers will soon begin to move to and fro as if floating in the liquid.

That sensation of floating will then change itself into a sensation of weightlessness, and the entire hand and the right forearm will begin to rise, higher and higher, as the balloon tugs and pulls on it.

The arm will bend at the elbow and the whole forearm will become vertical.

Then, you imagine another balloon tied to your right wrist and making the entire forearm and the arm weightless, from the tips of the fingers to the shoulder.

Your entire right arm will become increasingly more vertical, until the five minutes have elapsed.

Please concentrate on imagining the balloons and *do not* focus on your arm.

After the exercise is over, you will have ample time to recall whether the arm went up and, how high. One sure thing: If you keep imagining the balloon, that arm *will* go up.

Exercise Number 15:

Procedure

This is another in-hypnosis suggestion, so the procedure will be the same as in the previous exercise. The blueprint to be made *before* you put yourself to sleep will differ.

The in-hypnosis suggestion will be:

Glove anesthesia of one hand (either hand)

Time of hypnosis: preferably about 10 to 15 minutes

Blueprint to Submit to Subconscious Before Going Under

You imagine that, while you are under hypnosis, a doctor and a nurse are going to "work" on your hand by injecting it, from the wrist down to the tips of the fingers, with an anesthetic such as novocaine or spraying it with a volatile (cold-producing by rapid evaporation) liquid, such as carbon tetrachloride, keeping the hand immersed in salt ice water, which is much colder than standard ice water. Imagine that you feel the sensation of cold from the ice, or the displacement of the tissues by the injected anesthetic, the thickening of the skin as it becomes like a "leather glove" under the numbing effects of the chemicals "used" by the doctor and/or the nurse. You may imagine that the doctor is explaining how the anesthesia is being produced and perchance "hear" some of his words. You are mentally telling them which portions of your hand should be worked upon "some more" and urging them to do an even "better job." You could even imagine that the doctor is telling you the effect "is going to last a couple of minutes after you are awake," or until you think, in the waking state, three times "Everything is normal."

Note: *This last suggestion should preferably be left to a second or a third repetition of the exercise, when the effects have already proven satisfactory. Or you may simply make the image that the effect will terminate at the end of the self-hypnotic period.*

Exercise Number 16

Procedure

Here is another in-hypnosis exercise that should be done for five minutes, or even three minutes. The suggestion will be:

My hands are warm.

Blueprint to Submit to the Subconscious Before Going Under

During the hypnosis period, you will imagine that you are holding your hands in front of the flames of an open hearth, in an oven, under the rays of a sunlamp, or immersed in hot water, or alternately in any one of circumstances, or that your hands are subjected to any other form or sources of heat that you may imagine, and this for the full duration of the hypnotic period.

Exercise Number 17

Blueprint Optional

This will consist of *one* of the following suggestions, which you can regard as a small repertoire of training and entertaining exercises.

In each case, you imagine that during the hypnosis you will feel yourself in such circumstances as would produce the effect desired *if* they actually happened, which is simply a way of using your own printed circuits.

The suggestion could be one of the following:

1. My Feet Are Warm

Proposed image: your feet, nicely covered with woolen socks, are extended in front of a nice cozy fireplace, or resting on the open flap of the camp's pot belly stove.

2. My Feet Are Cold

Ice water pail, block of ice, ice bag, walking in snow, feet in the refrigerator, time when your feet really did freeze up on you, and so on.

3. My Hands Are Cold

Clearing windshield of snow, ice cubes, ice water pail, making snowballs with bare hand, and so on.

4. My Solar Plexus is Warm

Identify the spot at the fork of your lower ribs; use solar lamp, hot water bag or bottle, hot towel, and so on.

5. I Smell Roses—or other flower

You are walking in a garden of roses, stopping here and there to smell a particularly pleasant specimen. You pick up a rose and take it to your nose, inhaling the sweet odor, slow and deep.

6. Playing *Fantasia*

If you can "visualize easily" already—that is, see things in your mind's eye—have your subconscious "translate into images" for you a certain piece of music that plays while you go under. If you only "visualize" hazily thus far, the constant use of this exercise will enhance—quite rapidly—the clarity of your inner vision. If you cannot as yet see things with your eyes "closed," you should devote more time, later, to the exercises of Chapter 9. If you are musically inclined, you could produce the reverse type of *Fantasia* for yourself. That is, have your subconscious mind translate into sounds, melodies and arrangements some well-liked painting or scene. You could thus give yourself a sample of the method of inspiration used by Mozart, as related in Chapter 1.

Note: *You do not have to do more than any one of the exercises of this chapter before you pass on to the next. Exercises 14 or 15 should be sufficient, the rest can be considered optionals for future entertainment.*

CHAPTER 6

Time-Delayed Reactions

Training Yourself in Posthypnotic Suggestions

Definition

A posthypnotic suggestion is a suggestion that is given to the subconscious mind during hypnosis that is to be carried out by the subconscious —automatically—*after* the hypnotic period is over.

One Motivation Source

Automaticity is the trademark of the subconscious mind; the posthypnotic suggestion will be carried on whether the conscious mind likes it or not.

This is one way of actuating the precept of wisdom that says, "God grant me that I do the things I have to do, as I have to do, when I have to do them and whether I like to do them or not!"

The enforced accomplishment of a task under your own duress can evidently become a technique of self-motivation. It can be rather effective, but not quite as pleasant as the one that will be given in Chapter 8.

However, if this method appeals to your own psychological makeup, by all means use it.

Varieties of Posthypnotic Suggestions

Posthypnotic suggestions can be:

1. Keyed or unkeyed
2. Time-limited or continuous.

Keyed Suggestions

A posthypnotic suggestion is keyed when the performance suggested under hypnosis is to be carried out at a given signal—word, phrase, sentence, gesture, given place or hour of the day, and so on.

Examples of keyed suggestions are:

"Whenever you pick up a cigarette from your pack, you will . . ."

"Whenever I say 'Sleep now,' you will instantly go back into a deep hypnotic sleep . . ."

Limited Duration Suggestions

Frequently it is necessary or desirable to attach a time limit to the effects of a posthypnotic suggestion. This does not mean that if the operator "forgets" to provide a cancellation time for the suggestion, it will carry on "indefinitely."

Any posthypnotic suggestion is a form of conditioned reflex in which the need for repetition is reduced to a minimum, and one utterance is sometimes sufficient; still, it does not entirely escape the law of "a given number of times." The repetition of a hypnotic suggestion acts as a reinforcement; it produces the facilitation, the acceleration and amelioration of the performance, as already explained.

However, a posthypnotic suggestion that has no termination time included can, in certain cases, be quite annoying to the subject and even quite unethical.

Instances of time-limited posthypnotic suggestions are:

> "That pain in your gums will go away now, at the count of three, and disappear until Monday morning, at 10 o'clock, when you enter your dentist's office."

> "When you wake up, you will see the whole of this room as having a rosy color . . . until I say the word 'enough' . . ."

> A nonkeyed and non time-limited suggestion would be framed as follows: "In the future and beginning now, you will notice that you care less and less for the small irritations of life, such as . . ."

For training in self-hypnosis, the student will have little need for the concepts just given, but the details provided here may not be entirely useless.

First, the Suggestion

You already know that a suggestion is the writing of a printed circuit in the electronic brain of the subject.

Everyone acquainted with hypnosis quite readily understands the phenomenon of posthypnotic suggestions as they are given in hetero-hypnosis, where the "blueprint" is drafted by the "operator" for the subject.

Everyone understands that the operator can talk to the subject. But how can one talk to oneself when one is under hypnosis?

The answer is: "Don't talk to yourself while you are under hypnosis." In order to do so, you would have to play the dual roles of audience and actor. You would have to disrupt the relative positions of the subconscious and the conscious minds in hypnosis where, as Salter says, ". . . the subconscious mind comes to the fore with the expectation of being directed by the conscious mind of the operator . . ."

Do *not* talk to yourself while you are under hypnosis; just *imagine*, just make the images of what you want your subconscious mind to do and *make these images before* you put yourself under.

The image, the blueprint, is therefore made *before* going into hypnosis.

Four Techniques of Self-PHS (Posthypnotic Suggestion)

We will, in this chapter, elaborate four techniques for giving yourself posthypnotic suggestions.

We will describe each of these methods, then give instances of the application of each of them and, finally, apply each one of them to a specific academic problem, to the old bugaboo most commonly known as "My worst subject." The four methods are:

1. The mental pre-blueprint
2. The folded paper technique
3. The L-K-U-technique.
4. The tape recorder technique

PHS Technique Number One

Mental Blueprint Before Hypnosis

Let use suppose now that we want to transform into a posthypnotic suggestion the in-hypnosis suggestion that has been numbered Exercise Number 17, Option 5, "I smell the odor of roses."

In order to illustrate the technique of "mental blueprint before hypnosis," we will describe how to do it:

Exercise Number 18

You will put yourself "to sleep" for five minutes.

You will, in your mind's eye (and nose), during those five minutes, *imagine* yourself, in all kinds of circumstances, and *without* the real stimulus of a rose, smelling the odor of roses whenever you say to yourself, in the waking state, the following trigger sentence:

"Let me smell a rose," the order being given to the subconscious mind. Remember: The brain has always done the smelling job, whenever there was one to perform.

After the five minutes have elapsed, after you have thus imagined yourself smelling the odor of roses whenever you say to yourself the sentence-signal: "in all kinds of circumstances," on the bus (where it might become expedient), on the street, in your room, in the classroom, in the gym, while taking a shower, and so on, you can then test the PHS by actually using the key sentence to provoke the effect, automatically.

If the effect is not entirely to your liking, not "natural" or vivid enough, you can then do one of three things:

1. You can repeat the exercise, or
2. You can repeat Exercise Number 17, Option 5, and then test anew, or
3. You can "talk to George."

Talking to George

Talking to George is an interesting procedure that does serve to improve the responses of the subconscious mind to a given suggestion. It consists in letting George have it, in giving him a real pep talk, the "sergeant" type of talk, something like:

"Now, look here, George, when I tell you to let me smell the odor of roses, I mean that you r-e-a-l-l-y make me smell the odor of roses, you know what I mean, George? Now, let's do this over again, George, but, this time, give me the real McCoy, do you hear me, George?"

And, for all you know, George might very well answer you by doing the thing better the next time, as it has been experienced over and over again by a competent hypnotist.

Other Applications of This Technique

This same technique of giving yourself posthypnotic suggestions by the use of a previous blueprinting of the image, that image being the use of a posthypnotic key at will, in multiple circumstances, could now be applied to such suggestions as:

1. Whenever I think or say the sentence: "Balloon on my right wrist," I want that right hand to go up, as in Exercise 14, or
2. Whenever I say the phrase: "Right hand numb," I want that hand to be numb, or
3. Whenever I say or think the sentence: "My feet are cold," and so on.

It will readily be appreciated that such a technique, applied to a gradually increasing numbness in the pelvic area, forms the basis of training for painless childbirth.

PHS: Technique Number Two. The Folded-Paper Technique

In this technique of giving yourself posthypnotic suggestions, the image is made *before* you put yourself under hypnosis, as in all other cases where self-hypnosis is used.

In the "folded-paper technique," you write down the suggestion you want to give yourself, edit it in order to make it just as succinct as possible, fold the paper on which it has been edited, and hold that paper in your hand during the hypnotic period.

The folded paper acts as a trigger for the suggestion to be printed on the subconscious mind.

Suppose now you want to give yourself the suggestion expounded earlier: smelling a rose on cue.

You write down on a piece of paper the following suggestions:

1. Whenever I say or think to myself, anywhere, anytime, "Now let me smell the odor of roses," I do smell it just as if there were a rose under my nose.
2. You fold the paper neatly, hold it in one of your hands, and put yourself to sleep for a given number of minutes.
3. After the hypnotic period, and later at different moments, "in all kinds of circumstances," you use the key sentence and test George's obedience. Of course, you retain the same privilege of "talking to George" that you had in the previous instance and

that you have for all future needs. Do not underestimate the value of "bawling out George"; it can work wonders.

PHS Technique Number Three: The L-K-U Technique

The L-K-U technique of giving yourself post-hypnotic suggestions is, to our minds, the most efficient technique you can use.

It comprises three phases, as follows:

1. You live it under hypnosis.
2. You key it under hypnosis.
3. You test it in the waking state, and you then act according to the results, as indicated previously.

The most efficient application of the technique is to use it over and over again until the desired effect is obtained, if necessary working at it all day long and proving to yourself the statement of Emerson:

"A man *is* what he thinks about . . . all day long."

Suppose now we use this PHS Technique Number Three to produce an effect that may not be as useful in these times of abundance as it would have been to students of a previous generation: smelling the odor of steak at will.

Phase 1. You live it under hypnosis. You put yourself to sleep for five minutes *after* having made for yourself the following blueprint to "live" while under. You imagine the last time you received your monthly allowance through the mail, and gave yourself the full treatment at Joe's Cosmic Steak House, and then some.

You really want to smell that steak again as you relive the event and not only that one, but also the steak you had another time at Al's Rib Joint, and the time when . . . and the steak Ma used to serve and, in the same fashion, all the time when you smelled that appetizing, enchanting, palate-tingling aroma —in other words using all the printed circuits you may have in your mind about the odor of steak.

You really want to sense that smell in your mind's nostrils, because your nose never smelled it anyway. It was your brain: see Chapter 1.

Once you are satisfied that you have recaptured that divine scent, pass on to Phase 2.

Phase 2. You key it under hypnosis. Once more, you put yourself to sleep for five minutes and you want to see yourself—an image that you make *before* you go under—in all kinds of circumstances, even two days before your next allowance is due to arrive, using the key sentence: "Now, let me smell the odor of steak."

Phase 3: You use it in the waking state. You test it here and there, now and then, and, according to the results, you (a) repeat the whole schedule or (b) you talk to George.

PHS Technique Number Four: Tackling Your "Worst Subject"

The tape may be called the lazy man's hypnotist. The method consists merely of dictating the desired suggestion onto a magnetic tape and then listening to the suggestion while you are under hypnosis. It is not as efficient as Technique Number Three, but it can be useful in cases where visualization is poor.

If you were to go to a consulting hypnotist, with the express purpose of improving your "worst subject," he or she would first hypnotize you, and then, after making sure you respond to posthypnotic suggestions, the hypnotist would then tackle the problem of improving your worst subject by giving you a suggestion such as follows:

The Hypnotist's Suggestion

Now, we want to give the subconscious mind a very interesting suggestion regarding your worst subject which is X.

Every science, every subject was once your worst subject, because at one time or another in your life, you did not know a single thing about it.

Then, you were introduced to the subject, and because of the way the teacher presented it to you, or maybe because of the very personality of the teacher, you became interested in it and you found out that the subject was interesting to you and that interest, by itself, helped you acquire a measure of ability in that subject. Now regarding this subject X, it could be that the dislike and the distaste you have for it is somehow associated with something or someone.

It could be that the first teacher who introduced you to the subject lacked the proper pedagogical experience or maybe the proper knowledge of the subject. It could be that his or her personality was antagonistic or unpleasant.

It could be that your negative attitude to the subject X stems from hearsay, from attitudes of your family, from grade school days, or from other students.

It could be the failure of your first attempt was due to your lack of interest in the subject or to various other circumstances. No matter what associations may influence your present negative attitude toward the subject, is that a reason for accepting their influence in your present life?

Now, it becomes easy for you to think: "If I could develop some interest in subject X, that would certainly improve it." There is one fascinating source of interest in this subject for you: It is part of the whole picture of your scholastic (or academic) success and, as such, you are really interested in it. And that importance and interest of the subject now become stronger than any negative association that may tie in with it. After all, you know some people who excel in the subject, so that there must be something to it.

I want to find out, you might say to yourself, and I here and now resolve to find out what it is that interests them in subject X. Naturally, as you become more interested in subject X, you will find all sorts of occasions to improve your expertise in it. Maybe you will question some fellow students, maybe it would be wise to spend X minutes on it alone, daily.

You could use all or some of the idle moments of the day to do some mental rehearsing of the subject, you could recapitulate what you already know about the subject so as to launch you into a new beginning.

Maybe you could buy summaries, outlines, and booklets on it, and, of course, use them.

As you gradually become more interested in subject X, you naturally find that it becomes easier for you. As it becomes easier, you like it better and it becomes even easier.

Now you see yourself getting better grades in it. You can see yourself paying more attention in class and getting more out of the classes.

As a matter of fact, you *now* see yourself more interested in subject X, you see yourself getting better grades in it.

And, at the count of three, you will see yourself, in your mind's eye, doing just that and, by the end of one month, jumping two notches higher in this very subject X.

Now, let us take it from the mouth of the hypnotist and apply his or her suggestion to the four techniques of giving the same suggestion to yourself through self-hypnosis.

Exercise Number 19A: Ameliorating Your Worst Subject Using PHS Technique Number One:

You put yourself to sleep for five minutes and during those five minutes you want to imagine the following: You see yourself refusing to accept your previous conditionings to the fact that X is your worst subject.

You imagine how different things would have been had you not been conditioned negatively toward subject X.

You imagine yourself interested in the subject *because* it is part of the total picture of your academic success.

You imagine yourself being (not becoming) more interested in the subject and taking all opportunities to expose yourself to it.

You imagine yourself requesting the help of some fellow students, every day, at an appointed hour and for so many minutes.

You see yourself getting better grades in it *every week* and jumping two notches in your grades on a certain date (e.g., one month from date of first exercise) with that date remaining the same throughout your hypnotic campaign toward improving subject X.

Exercise Number 19B: Ameliorating Your Worst Subject Using PHS Technique Number Two

You begin by editing the suggestion of the hypothetical hypnotist given on page 88 in the following manner, and you write it down on a piece of paper, which you can fold neatly to hold in your hand:

You are now dumping all negative conditionings regarding subject X.

You are interested in subject X *because* it is part of the whole picture of your academic success.

Therefore, X becomes easier as you take immediate steps to improve in it.

Every day, no matter what time you go to bed, you spend *one hour* working on subject X, reviewing, practicing, and questioning yourself on it.

You use all possible aids to improve X and, on such a date (put in date), you will be two grades better in subject X.

Exercise Number 19C: Ameliorating Your Worst Subject Using PHS Technique Number Three

Phase One: You live it under hypnosis, for five minutes as in Technique One, on page 91.

Phase Two: Under hypnosis, and for five minutes, you see yourself, every night before you go to sleep, working one hour on subject X and being unable to go to sleep until you have done so.

Phase Three: If you find you can go to sleep without studying subject X for one hour, use alternatives already given on page 88.

Exercise Number 19D: Ameliorating Your Worst Subject Using PHS Technique Number Four:

In applying this technique to the problem of your worst subject, the solution is rather simple. You simply dictate the suggestion the hypnotist would have used in such a case with an actual student and then listen to it while you are under hypnosis, by the very simple expedient of having a long enough lead on your tape to give you the time to take your usual posture and put yourself to sleep.

Some Additional Testing

In order to satisfy yourself that you do possess self-hypnosis, you may use *one* of the following posthypnotic suggestions:

1. When I wake up, I will feel an urge to pick up such and such a book.
2. When I wake up, I will feel an urge

to take such and such a walk (not
habitual).

In the preceding chapter, we gave a list of
in-hypnosis suggestions in which all the effects
were sensorial. That was done to avoid the frequent objection: "I wonder whether I was not
doing it all on my own accord."

So far in this chapter, except for the suggestions regarding your "worst subject," we have
done the same because you cannot produce "on
your own accord" the proposed sensorial responses.

Those last two exercises will then be less subject to the usual doubts about the validity of
the effects.

PART THREE:

Utilizing Self-Hypnosis
as a Student*

---

*If you have now sat down to the task of acquiring
self-hypnosis, do *not* practice the exercises of this
third section *unless* you have passed the second
part of this book.

CHAPTER 7

Improving Your Concentration, Your Memory, and Your Learning Tools

The Tools of the Student

Beyond the financial means to take college courses and the motivation to succeed, some of the essential tools of the student are:

Concentration during lectures and at study time

Some memory training

Rapid reading

The art of learning

Though rapid reading and the art of learning are beyond the scope of this book, some methods of improving them through the aid of self-hypnosis will be given in this chapter.

Memory

Memory is the faculty of recall of a previously printed bit or sequence of information. It is the

97

expression of an already impressed amount of data in the memory bank of your electronic brain, called the subconscious mind.

As has already been seen, the conscious mind is merely the operator that reads the dials, once the internal computer has scanned for the desired material.

If someone asks you for your home address, that information immediately springs to your conscious mind, but your conscious mind was not aware of that information until the question acted as a stimulus for the subconscious mind to start scanning, in the vast warehouse of its imprinted information, that tiny bit of information.

In a flash, the computer projected the data onto the screen of your conscious mind, which immediately read the dials and became aware: "My home address is such-and-such."

Three Phases

Memory is a three-phase phenomenon and those three phases are:

1. The printing of a "viveogram."
2. The storage or retention of the information.
3. The recall.

Printing

Obviously, the most important part of the process is the printing itself, and that printing, in turn, depends upon the following factors:

1. Your interest in the material to be retained.

2. Your will to retain it.
3. The vividness or originality of the printing.
4. The lack of interference (concentration) at the moment of printing.
5. The richness of the mental associations between the impressed material and the materials already printed in the machine.
6. The number of repetitions of the printing.

In the measure that one or some of the previously mentioned factors are increased, in the very same measure the other factors may be decreased.

The object of the ideal method of study is to do away, as much as possible, with factor number 6, repetition.

Retention

The storage of the material learned is automatic; that is, it never erases itself from the subconscious mind, as has already been demonstrated by the Penfield experiments.

Nevertheless it can be enhanced by the organization of the material absorbed into a larger whole and the lack of interference to retention. It is a basic tenet of psychology that the subconscious will repress events, bits of events, or any one or series of "engrams" to ensure a better equilibrium of the whole personality.

Such a subconscious "refusal to print or store information" may quite naturally be present in the psychological makeup of any given student.

Recall

Evidently the most practical aspect of memory, recall is directly proportional to the amount of "wanting" to remember a given bit of information and inversely proportional to the lack of interference at the moment where the bit of information is needed.

Such interferences as anxiety, nervousness, old patterns of "failure wishing," and the generally expected attack of the jitters at examination time are commonly associated with lack of concentration.

Concentration can be defined as the freedom from interferences at the moment of execution of a given task.

It is considered as the capacity of so absorbing oneself into a given occupation that the mind and the senses are closed to any other object of attention.

Everyone has had those moments of concentration, at the movies, while reading a captivating novel and identifying with the hero or heroine, while watching TV, reading, working.

Everyone knows the classical instance of the college professor working out a problem while mentally he or she steps in the mud or the rain puddle.

It should not, however, be mistaken for daydreaming, when the conscious mind is simply glued to the unrolling of the inner film of associated ideas, which is often called thinking.

Concentration is the act of converging something toward a center, such as the light rays under the covering power of a lens. Mental concentration is also the act of returning to a center of interest.

It is surprising that so many people complain about their lack of concentration during study and yet never point to the lack of concentration in their own daily lives.

Quite evidently, concentration, or returning to a given center of interest, clearly applies to the habit (or the lack of it) of focusing one's life efforts and one's interests toward a given goal or set of goals.

Because concentration is so important to memory, the two are generally tied in together into a single suggestion.

However, because in our belief, either can be developed separately (but necessarily profiting the other), we will give separate techniques of developing concentration and memory through self-hypnosis.

Exercise Number 20: Intensifying Your Concentration

We will begin by giving the suggestion as a consulting hypnotist would give it to a subject:

We have all seen instances of people being so absorbed by whatever they were doing, whether it is working, reading, or studying, that nothing, absolutely nothing seemed to disturb them. We have all seen people so focused on the tasks at hand that nothing seemed able to call their attention beyond what they were doing. We have all seen cases of people so engrossed in what they were doing that they did not hear the doorbell or the ring of the telephone.

We have all seen cases of people so concentrated on what they were doing that neither voices nor noises nor movements of people around them could attract their mind—so concentrated, as a matter of fact, that people had to nudge them a few times before succeeding in contacting them.

You may even remember such a moment of total absorption in what you were doing that no one and nothing for a time could bring you out of it.

Now, beginning today, whenever and wherever you say to yourself aloud, or think to yourself: "Now, concentration until such and such a time . . .," you will immediately become so engrossed, so focused, and so interested in what you are doing, whether it be reading, studying, or attending a class, that your mind will then be closed to anything else.

Whenever and wherever you say those words to yourself, orally or mentally, you become so concentrated that no interferences from the outside, such as voices or noises of movements in your visual range can disturb you and no interferences from the inside, such as itches or twitches of the body, no thoughts or feelings will disturb you.

And you will find that, as soon as you use those words: "Now, concentration until such and such a time . . .," everything prints itself more vividly and more deeply on your subconscious mind.

You will find that whatever you know about the subject flows freely to your conscious mind and that the information is thus much better integrated with what you previously knew about it. Better still, you will find yourself so integrating the information absorbed that you will quite often surprise yourself by projecting what you are then learning into its natural and logical conclusions and foresee some of the things you will be learning later on the same subject.

You will find that your newfound concentration gives you a feeling of active participation and thorough assimilation of the knowledge absorbed.

Of course, this new intense concentration makes for a better printing of the material on your subconscious mind and you will find that, whenever some piece of information could be useful to you at that moment, it will spring to your mind like water gushes out of a source, whether you need that information for discussing a subject, mentally brushing up on it, or giving a lecture or writing an examination.

And the hypnotist would now add:

Now, at the count of three, you will see yourself, over and over again, and in all kinds of circumstances, using that key for better concentration.

At the count of *three*, you will see yourself using the key sentence: "Now, concentration until such and such a time . . .," and as soon as you say those words to yourself, you will see yourself so engrossed, so focused, so interested, so concentrated that your mind and your senses are closed, but totally closed, to whatever goes on around you and to any other thought or feeling but the matter at hand.

And you will see yourself doing just that, beginning today, for the coming week or fortnight, just so long, as a matter of fact, as it would take in actual life to make it a habit—a habit for the conscious mind to use the key and a habit for the subconscious mind to produce the effect.

Now, you begin to see yourself using your

new key for total concentration: One, two, three . . .

Choose Your Technique

The student will have readily perceived that the full text just given could be used for tape method of PHS.

Also, it is seen just as readily that the part beginning with "Now, you will see yourself . . ." (on page 103), is equivalent to the first technique of PHS, the pre-blueprinting method.

To use the L-K-U technique of PHS, the student would proceed as follows:

1. *See* himself or herself so absorbed, when studying, listening to a class or lecture, observing for the purpose of learning, that nothing else interferes, thus better assimilating everything he or she absorbs, having all useful material at hand whenever discussing, talking about or writing on whatever has been previously studied.
2. He or she would then *see* himself or herself using the key signal "Now, concentration until . . .," over and over again, projecting the use of such a key into the future.
3. Use the key in actual life and according to the results, start over again from step 1.

If the student prefers the folded-paper technique, he or she would start by editing the long formula unto a piece of paper and then proceed with the previously described method (Chapter 6).

Note: *Evidently, if the student has not yet acquired the use of vivid mental imagery, he or she should be content with* imagining *the actions and attitudes described, or use a PHS technique that does not require mental visualization.*

Improving Your Memory

Mnemonic Methods

All mnemonic methods make use of two properties of the human mind: the laws of association of ideas or sound and the structuring needs of the mind.

Numerous books have been written on the subject of acquiring a "memory like that of an elephant." Whatever the retentive capacity of the well-known pachyderm, we will here give a general synopsis of the methods extant in those diverse courses and systems.

We will now briefly elaborate on the preceding material so that students may become interested in reading a good book (just as good as any "correspondence course") on the subject.

$$
\text{Association of ideas}
\begin{cases}
\text{Link}
\begin{cases}
\text{1. Homophony} \\
\text{2. Associative chains}
\end{cases} \\
\text{Hook}
\begin{cases}
\text{3. Number codes} \\
\text{4. Mental hooks} \\
\text{5. Numbered mental cardex}
\end{cases}
\end{cases}
$$

$$
\text{Structuring}
\begin{cases}
\text{6. Wholing images} \\
\text{7. Mental architecturing}
\end{cases}
$$

Homophony

This is most valuable in the study of languages and a few examples will be given as applied to the acquisition of a vocabulary in a given language.

The Spanish word for "to yawn" is *bostezar*. If you think of a mouth that busts, could it not easily remind you that "yawning" is bost . . . ezar?

"Road" is *carretera* in Spanish. What about associating the homophonic link: "Roads are made for carr . . . iages"?

"Iron," in French, is *fer*. Of course, you know that iron is a fair . . . ly useful metal, and by making the homophonic link, you can easily remember the word.

A "mirror," in Italian is *uno specchio*. An easy homophonic link would be: "a mirror is a device in which you can see "spec . . . tres."

Thus, a daily diet of so many words, listed at each end of a given line—with the appropriate homophonic links in between can, in a very brief period of time, give you a vocabulary of

1,000 words, one thousand being merely 50 times 20.

Here is a brief example of such a list:

> Blue—blue eyes can be a "soul inspiring" —*Azul*
>
> Walk—walk in, come in, cam in—*Caminar*
>
> Date—(of day) to find it—fetch a calendar —*Fecha*

Puns, quasi-alliterations, roundabout phrases, all can be helpful to the student who wants to associate a word in his or her own language to another word in a given idiom.

The Number Code

Because of its extensive applications and merits, however, we will stop for a moment on the familiar (to the students of mnemonics) technique of the number code.

It consists in translating the entire alphabet into numbers, so that numbers (such as for dates and quantities) can be translated into sentences or logical links with the material to be retained.

Without entering into any justification for the code itself, we will content ourselves with giving the code that is used in all systems and dates back several hundred years.

The code is easy to memorize and will repay a thousandfold such time as you may have to spend on learning it by rote.

T or D	are 1
N	is 2
M	is 3
R	is 4
L	is 5

J, Sh, Ch	are 6
K, hard G, Q	are 7
Ph, F, or V	are 8
P or B	are 9
Z or S	are 0

Conventions—Vowels have no numerical value, double consonants count as a single consonant.

It can readily be seen that, according to our code, one can easily retain the fact that the cranium contains 26 bones, "because" it is the *niche,* n representing 2 and the *ch* in the same word "meaning" 6.

All dates of history can also be remembered by making up a sentence, the first syllable of each word giving a digit in the full date, or by a single word that somehow recalls the event. Of course, the full sentence is the more flexible method.

For instance, 1513 is the date when Balboa discovered the Pacific Ocean by crossing the isthmus of Panama and established the fact that the West Indies were not the East Indies but merely an obstacle on the road to them.

Rather then memorize the arid number 1513 as being the date of the event, one could form a sentence logically linking the date with the event. For instance, "The long trip meant something: The Indies were not the Indies."

Wholing Images

One last element of mnemonics that will be discussed briefly because it is presented in most books or systems of memory training is the wholing image.

It can best be described by giving an example.

Suppose you have to correlate the events, which, in 1789, catalyzed the French Revolution. The sequence of events, in that fateful year, is:

The meeting of the Estates-General, the third estate transforming the meeting into a National Assembly, suspended for three days, when the members of the Commons pronounce the oath of the Tennis Court; the storming of the Bastille, the abolition of the privileges and the return of the king.

The events are solidly related by an unusual drawing in which, in the background, two generals, representing the Estates, are playing handball, and the generals in the foreground are taking "pastilles" (homophony) from a bowl next to a sign saying "National Assembly"; at the foot of the sign is the heap of scrapped privileges, the king, Louis XVI, trudging back home.

All such techniques can of course be used concomitantly. For example, words taken from a mental catalog could have been introduced into the preceding image to represent the actual dates of the events tied in by the "wholing image."

The mental catalog is a series of one hundred noun-images, generally made up through the use of the number code. The mental catalog is then committed to memory and can be used for all the multiple uses of memorizing events, names, dates, and so on.

Whatever your decision about using or not using the existing systems of mnemonics, memory can be increased independently of them by suggestion.

Exercise Number 21:
Improving Your Memory

As we have done for the exercise on amelio-
rating concentration, we will start here by giving the suggestion as a practicing hypnotist
would phrase it to a client.

It is assumed at this stage that the student is
sufficiently well versed in the application of the
four methods of practicing posthypnotic suggestions as to be able to deduce the way in
which the hypnotist's verbatim suggestions can
be used for each separate method.

Therefore, the other three methods of PHS
will only be briefly commented on.

Here is then the full suggestion for upgrad-
ing your memory:

"You now have a greatly improved memory,
for many reasons."

"You are more interested in retaining everything."

"You are more interested in remembering what
you study and you are more interested in remembering events and people, because it all
makes for a more interesting life."

"In fact, you are so interested in remembering that you regularly practice this suggestion
for a better memory and the exercise for inten-
sifying your concentration."

"All obstacles that so far may have influenced
your memory are now fading away, whatever
they may be. No more are you affected by associating such and such a subject with the personality of the professor teaching it, or the sup-
posed dryness of the subject. All subconscious
wishes to spite someone or punish yourself,

all negative conditionings are just melting away."

"You *know* that everything you read, hear, or study is printed in your subconscious mind, that nothing is ever erased from the inner memory bank."

"Everything you learn is now better printed because you organize it better in your mind, because you associate better what you learn with what you already know."

"You use natural and artificial associations, such as memory techniques, and your interest and your concentration at the moment are the absorption of knowledge, which makes for a much more vivid impression of the material."

"You enjoy regular and periodical reviews and recapitulations of the material you have to learn. You regularly practice "shadow questioning," which is comparable to shadow boxing: you regularly and mentally question yourself, during your free moments, by putting such questions to yourself as an examining professor would do."

"Whenever you need any bit of information, whether for discussing a subject, reviewing it, or giving a lecture on it, or writing on it, it springs naturally to your mind, just like water gushes from the source."

"No more fretting or fuming when you are trying to recall something; you merely think to yourself: 'Now, let me remember such-and-such a thing,' and it is there and then springs to your mind."

"Whenever and wherever you have use for a given bit of knowledge, the very need for that material makes you calm and easy."

"Whether it be in the classroom, in the lecture hall, or sitting for an examination, we repeat, the mere *need* for the bit of information or knowledge makes you feel at ease, calm, and self-possessed, because you *know* you now have a better memory."

"And when you count to three, you will *see* yourself, for the rest of this period of hypnotic sleep, in all kinds of circumstances, either studying, reviewing, or sitting for any subject, you will be more interested, use better concentration, better associations, and feel calm and self-possessed whenever and wherever you need to recall something."

"One, Two, Three . . ."

Rapid Reading

Reading

Reading is the active process of closing the communication gap between a supposedly worthy author and a supposedly interested interlocutor.

It aims at the transfer of ideas, facts, feelings, not of *words*.

It is the process of connecting the mind of the author and the mind of the reader. It is carried on through the eyes of the reader but not *by* his or her eyes.

Reading should be the grasping of facts, ideas, data, or feelings but not of words.

Reading, unlike listening, need not be a slow-motion process. In listening, the time element necessary for articulating words is inherently inevitable. Ideas have to be reconstructed as they emerge from their sound shells.

Not necessarily so in reading, where the pristine, unfettered transmission of thought can compete with the telegraphic celerity of an Indian saying: "Me scalp you."

There are only a few individuals who have the ability to instantaneously extract ideas from the core of words in which they were imbedded.

Today, this process is at the beck and call of almost everyone; it is called *rapid reading*.

Definition

Rapid reading is just that process of reading for ideas and not for words.

It is the most active and can be the most exhilarating method of digesting that more or less considerable unit of knowledge, information, or entertainment that has been called a book, an article, and so on.

Clearly then, rapid reading could best be described as reading for ideas. Its most succinct formula would therefore be to detect the flow of thoughts.

From that single necessity of its definition, all the procedures for rapid reading can be deduced.

Grammatically speaking, ideas are expressed by paragraphs, a paragraph being the fully clothed expression of an idea which can, however, be expressed in the Indian's telegraphic style. To do any form of rapid reading, one must get used to looking for those words that are the skeletal members of the paragraph. Those are called *key words*.

Key words are "idea flow directing" or "idea skeleton-forming" words; that is, they may be

directing the traffic, or they may be the very
vehicles (parts of ideas) in transit.

Reading Signposts

Some "traffic-directing" words indicate that
there are no turns, no bends, no obstacles in
the flow of thought.

They include such words as:

    And
    More
    Moreover
    More than that
    Furthermore
    Also
    Likewise

Some traffic-directing words are turnabout
words. They indicate that the flow of thought is
changing. They include such words as:

    But
    Yet
    Nevertheless
    Although
    Despite
    In spite of
    On the contrary
    However
    Notwithstanding
    Rather
    Still

Quite often, they indicate that an author is
dismissing what he or she has explained before
as unworthy of anything but rejection.

Some traffic words are the concluding, final-
izing, or summarizing words:

    Thus
    So
    And so

Therefore
Consequently
Accordingly
In conclusion
As a result
Finally
Concluding
In short

Among the *idea-forming* words, nouns—names, dates, numbers—and verbs are the most important.

The Role of the Eyes

As a natural consequence of the intention of rapid reading—reading for ideas—the eye must break its habit of reading word for word.

This involves reforming two of the main teachings of reading: increasing the eye span and conditioning a new habit of eye rhythm.

The eye span is increased by the use of such tools as the tachistoscope, and the eye rhythm is obtained gradually by practicing, for a while, nothing but the rapid scanning of a column of text by doing two fixations per line.

Even without any machine, a determined student will develop the knack of going down a newspaper column (now less than two inches) first with two fixations per line and eventually with one fixation per line.

He will thus have trained his eyes in absorbing the number of words contained on the average by a column of newspaper text.

By coupling this practice with that of excluding one or two "flow-directing words" each and every time they are met with in a text, as fast as possible and then faster again, the average

student should be able to double his or her
reading speed within six weeks.

Once adept at these two exercises, the student need only add constant practice: continuous and active restructuring of the author's
"idea flow" as he or she reads.

In other words, as the student reads, there is
constantly in his or her mind the preoccupa-
tion: "What is the author saying? How does he
make his point? How does this paragraph or
those last two or three paragraphs fit in with
the development of his ideas?"

Obviously, such thoughts are not expressed
in words in the reader's mind, but they are
constantly present in his mind as he reads.

The more and ever-present focusing of the
mind on the task of extracting the flow of ideas
from a given text will automatically result in a
much more rapid reading technique.

Thus, even without any formal training in
rapid reading, an effective posthypnotic suggestion can be made for improving your reading skill and speed.

And such is the aim of the following exercise.

Exercise Number 22: Increasing Your Reading Speed and Efficiency

As has already been said, we will merely give
the suggestion as it would be given by a hypnotist upon request, and the student is expected
to adapt this verbatim text to his or her own
method of PHS.

We all know that the natural tendency of the
mind is to grasp ideas as a whole.

"Now, rapid reading is that very method of reading that consists of reading for ideas, and not having the mind slowed down by the unnecessary words that make up sentences.

"Therefore, the mere fact of wanting to read faster will prompt you to overlook the unnecessary trimmings and unravel the ideas contained in the written text.

"As a matter of fact, trainees in rapid reading are taught to will and wish and try to read faster.

"As of now, you read faster and yet you grasp more of what you read because you want to read faster and you read for ideas.

"You have the knack of extracting ideas from the mass of words in which they are imbedded.

"As you read, you are more active than ever, constantly pressing yourself to follow the thread of thought that the writer is unwinding.

"Key words, traffic-directing words, and the idea-forming words, just spring to your eyes as you read.

"Dates, names, numbers interest you more than ever and your eyes are constantly on the lookout for them.

"Every day you train your eyes in reading a newspaper column in one or two fixations, and your eye span and speed thus become greater every day.

"Whenever you read anything, it is now a habitual practice for you to review an article and a chapter or part of a chapter *immediately* after you have finished reading it.

"And, as you read faster, you also read with

more pleasure because you grasp and retain more, as you now read for ideas and for data, according to the nature of the text.

"And now, at the count of three . . ."

CHAPTER 8

Self-Motivation:
The Bootstrap Operation

The Eternal Trinity of Success

If magicians could grant wishes, and if you happened to meet one at a party, you could do no better than to ask for the fulfillment of three wishes:

1. A worthy goal.
2. The removal of the obstacles to that goal.
3. A powerful and relentless impetus toward that goal.

Of course, each and every student already has the first element of the eternal trinity of success—a goal—and that goal is academic success, whether it be expressed as a diploma or simply "passing grades."

Every hypnotist or psychologist who has ever worked with students knows that the most common complaints are: lack of concentration, inadequate memory, and procrastination, lack of discipline and method-in-studying.

These considerations leave us with two of the elements of academic success to treat: (1) the obstacles and (2) the regularity of motivation to action toward success.

These two problems will constitute the object of this chapter.

Your Number One and Number Two Private Enemies

The need to do away with procrastination or "Operation taking the lead out" singles out the student's Private Enemy Number One.

Lack of working discipline is another one, and we would seem to have named them all by adding the traditional "slump," that well-known symptom of "the wish to fail" that everyone complains of at times.

However, those obstacles are different facets of one and the same thing: subconscious obstacles to success. One may wish to fail academically for a full variety of unconscious reasons—to spite someone, most often the parents who are occasionally consciously accused of imposing their own aims in life upon their offspring; a hidden guilt complex, a "dependency complex" or even unadulterated laziness, whether inherited or acquired.

The student's Private Enemy Number Two is academically termed "lack of motivation."

We will now proceed to give a formula of post-

hypnotic suggestion for each of those private
enemies of the student.

Conscious and Subconscious Obstacles
to Success

The exercise we are about to formulate is
borrowed from psychoanalytical and hypnoan-
alytical techniques called *desensitization.*

For the average person, it can have just as
much value as months of psychoanalysis.

It is equally applicable to the removal of the
obstacles to your academic success and to a
severe case of "the slumps," as well as to a
fortuitous state of despondency.

It is called the "cloud and sun exercise." It
consists in visualizing a cloud that symbolizes
the obstacles of the moment or the habitual
obstacles to free and functional living.

Over and above the cloud, one imagines—and
preferably visualizes a sun—dim and hazy at
first, but slowly and gradually gaining in strength
—and that sun symbolizes the will to live, the
desire to have a free and happy life.

We repeat: The cloud and sun exercise is tremendously fertile in applications, and the fact
that it is specifically designed to eliminate the
obstacles to academic success should not prevent the student from using it in all cases where
a temporary "obstacle to living free" is present.

Exercise Number 23: The Cloud and Sun Exercise

As we already began to do in the last chapter, we will only give the verbatim suggestion a hypnotist would deliver for the purpose at hand, and students will then apply the given text to the specific method of giving themselves post-hypnotic suggestions they prefer.

The hypnotist would say something such as: "Now, at the count of three, I want you to imagine a cloud, a cloud hovering over and about you, and when you do imagine that cloud in such a fashion that you could almost swear you can see it with your mind's eye, I want you to move the little finger of the right hand.

"One, Two, Three . . .

"Good! (when the little finger or any other pre-chosen finger moves).

"Now I want you to think of that cloud as representing all the obstacles to your own success in life or in college.

"I want you to think of that cloud as symbolizing all the negative thoughts, all the negative attitudes, and all the negative conditionings of your life.

"I want you to imagine that this cloud represents all the frustrations, all the rebuttals, all the previous ideas of failure or shortcomings, all the negative assertions from other people that may yet influence you.

"I want you to think of that cloud and feel that it represents all the subconscious reasons you may harbor for spiting someone in your life, whether it is your parents or some professor; I want you to think and feel about that cloud as if it represents any of your subconscious reasons for failing or punishing yourself. That cloud also symbolizes all past negative habits of procrastination or laziness.

"Now, over and beyond that cloud, if you will notice carefully, there is a sun, a sun that may be hazy and dim for a while, but you can feel it is there.

"Now, that sun represents your will to live, your desire to lead a freer, richer, and more abundant and successful life.

"Now, that sun *is* there, or else you would not be doing this exercise now. And as you, as a witness to this process, side with that sun, you will presently see sunshine through that cloud, first pushing a shaft of light here and there and gradually making that cloud lift and evaporate.

"Now that sun begins to work on that cloud and, as it does so, you get the feeling of good riddance, as if a load were taken off your shoulders.

"Now, as you watch that cloud and the sun working to make it lift and evaporate, you feel that you are free of the obstacles that thus far have prevented you from enjoying academic success and a free and happy life.

"Now, during the rest of this period of hypnotic sleep, that sun will so radiate its rays on the cloud that you will finally see it completely dispel that cloud, like the mist of the morning under the rays of the rising sun.

"You will finally see that sun burst through after having dispelled the cloud and you will then feel as if you were basking in the light of that sun.

"You will feel the rays of that sun so vividly

impinging upon the skin of your body that you can almost feel the pricking of those rays. And those rays will bear names; some will be marked 'Success,' others 'Enthusiasm,' others 'Self-confidence,' others 'Assurance,' others 'Concentration,' others 'Powerful memory'—still other rays will bear the names of all the qualities you want in your own life.

"And you will feel yourself so impregnated, so soaked with those rays that you will know that, upon waking up, you will be radiating those rays in your turn. And you will be able to do this exercise, wherever and whenever you so desire, for any given number of minutes or seconds, by merely thinking to yourself:

"Now, I will do the Sun Exercise for so many minutes," and then counting from one to twenty.

"And you will find that, each and every time, the cloud is thinner and smaller, till finally it is only the light fog of the negative feelings of the day.

"And this process will go on till the end of this timed exercise, when you will wake up feeling well and refreshed and fully charged with the success qualities of that sun."

The preceding exercise has been used over the years by the author and it can definitively be asserted, through experience, that it works—splendidly. Make your profit of it by using it abundantly.

Exercise Number 24: The Burning of the Leaves

Another exercise for "eliminating the negative" is one that we will call the "burning of the leaves."

It can be of the same value as the previous one, which has been named the "cloud and sun exercise," and it is given here as a matter of possible preference by the student.

Needless to say Exercise Number 24 is an alternative to Exercise Number 23, and the two need not be used by students for the purpose of eliminating what we have termed and discussed as "the obstacles to success."

Once more, we only give the verbatim suggestion the hypnotist would use, and the student is expected to apply the contents of the suggestion to the specific posthypnotic suggestion technique he or she prefers.

The hypnotist would then say:

"I want you to imagine yourself, at the count of three, in a garden, a garden that might symbolize the "garden of your life," and when you do imagine yourself in that garden, I want you to let me know by moving the thumb of your right (or left) hand.

"One, Two, Three . . .

"Good (when he sees the specified finger moving).

"Now, this is the garden of your life, and, if you look carefully around, you will notice here and there dried leaves which lie about that garden.

"Now, those dried and undesirable leaves symbolize all the frustrations, all the humiliations, all the negative happenings of your life, all the negative conditionings such as feelings of inferiority, feelings of inadequacy, all refusals, all rebuttals, all negative statements about yourself that anyone might have made at any time in your life.

"I want you now to use a rake, which is there somewhere in the garden, and collect all those leaves into a heap and set fire to them. You could put names on some of those leaves; some of them might represent disagreeable events in your life, some of them might represent subconscious wishes for failure; some of them might represent opinions or dislikes for some professor or other authority figure in your life.

"Some of those leaves might represent past negative conditionings, procrastination, laziness; some of them might represent any spite you might hold against anyone, whoever they may be. Whatever those leaves might symbolize, they have to be burned out of your life, out of the garden of your life, and, as you set fire to them, I want you to enjoy their deliberate destruction. I want you to feel the feeling of liberation and riddance as you stamp them underfoot and as you see them turned into ashes or fly away under the wind.

"And I want you to go around that garden of your life, pick up all those leaves, and burn them in that bonfire.

"And you take a real pleasure in gathering the very last of those leaves and setting fire to the lot.

"And, when the time is over, you will wake up, feeling fine and refreshed and as if a load has been taken off your shoulders."

Exercise Number 25: Making Self-Discipline Pleasurable

Once more, we simply give the verbatim suggestion a hypnotist would use for such a purpose and leave it to the student to apply it to the specific posthypnotic technique of his or her choice:

You have now eliminated the obstacles to your own success, so that you can feel free to build anew and facilitate your own life as a student.

You now take pleasure in doing your hypnotic exercises for concentration, memory, and rapid reading.

It is now a pleasure for you to take the steps useful toward your academic success.

The things you have to do for succeeding in your studies, you now undertake with pleasure, even if some people should call it discipline and shun it or deride it.

You set aside, daily and weekly, periods of time for studying and applying the self-hypnotic tools you have acquired.

You now have and enjoy the habit of reviewing your material so that you assimilate it with ease and efficiency.

Weekly periods of reviewing are now habitual with you and monthly periods or recapitulation are so natural to you that you could not care less for anything else until those are done.

All subjects interest you because they are all part of your academic success.

By disciplining yourself and alloting time for every task, you find you have more time for extracurricular or social activities. You constantly feel the urge to assimilate your daily quota of subject matter and you enjoy this as an insurance policy of success.

Now, at the count of Three, and until the time for this hypnotic period is over, I want you to see yourself doing your hypnotic exercises regularly, according to a schedule, daily assimilating your quota of subject matter for the day, weekly reviewing and monthly recapitulating your subjects and enjoying it all.

One, Two, Three . . .

Willpower Versus Goal Power

It is a moot question whether there exists such an entity as that called willpower.

It has even been argued pro and con whether there exists that which has been called free choice. It has been held that, even in that primordially important question, free choice is nothing but the result of the greater attraction of one out of many alternatives.

In either case, it is a well-known psychological fact that, because humans are goal-seeking animals, a sufficiently attractive goal will supply the necessary motivation to attain it where willpower by itself is subject to all the vagaries of its own want of definiteness.

It seems, in fact, that willpower is a by-product of goal power and that it springs from the pressure of the goal in the same fashion as the pressure in your tap springs from the pressure of the head of water in your local reservoir or the applied pressure of the pumps that distribute the water to consumers.

The following exercise has proven most useful as the solution to the oft-expressed need of "taking the lead out."

Two alternate suggestions are here given, so that one or the other might serve the student, according to whether or not he or she can "visualize."

That is, the alternate exercises, Numbers 25A and 25B may be used, the latter by those students who cannot as yet "see things" with their eyes closed and the former by those who do have that capacity.

Such a procedure has been adopted because some readers may or may not proceed beyond this chapter; mental visualization seems an insuperable obstacle to some, and others may not have the resolve to spend the time and effort involved in acquiring it.

Exercise Number 25A: Taking the Lead Out

For the Visualizers

At the count of Three, I want you to see something very interesting.

At the count of Three, you will see *two* films of yourself in five years from now.

You may see those two films side by side, or you may see them one after the other, but you will see two films of yourself five years from now (or at the end of your academic studies) according to whether you use or do not use the tools that have been given to you thus far.

You have been given tools for increasing your concentration, your memory, and your learning abilities.

You have been given tools whereby you can adhere to a working discipline in your life as a student.

At the count of Three, I want you to see a film that shows you what success you have attained *if* you use those tools and have used more than the traditional ten percent of your capabilities. On the other film, you will see yourself and the success you obtain if you do *not* use the tools that have been provided for you.

One, Two, Three . . .

Exercise Number 25B: Taking the Lead Out

For the Nonvisualizers

You know that, according to William James, the average person does not use more than 10 percent of his or her capabilities.

Now, you have been given tools that permit you to escape the law of average and get a few points better than the normal 10 percent.

You have been given tools whereby you can increase your concentration and your memory; you have been given tools that will facilitate for you the task of learning and achieving success.

Now, at the count of Three, I want you to imagine how much you can benefit, over the years and at graduation time, from using those tools you have been equipped with.

At the count of Three, I want you to imagine

all the time and effort you can save for yourself and the improvement you can make in your life, both academically and otherwise, by using those tools.

At the count of Three, and for the duration of this exercise, I want you to imagine how much easier and better your life can be if you use those tools regularly. *As of now*, I want you to decide that you *are* using them, regularly and beginning *now*.

One, Two, Three . . .

CHAPTER 9

Sleep Learning Without Machines

Free Night Shift

It is surprising that the use of self-hypnosis for putting "George" to work during the hours of natural sleep is not more widespread.

For years, hypnoanalysis has been used for suggesting to patients that "sometime during the next few days, you will have a dream that will bear on this problem, and we will then work together on interpreting that dream."

Of course, this is tantamount to saying that nonmedical hypnosis has a long way to go.

Yet, that capacity for using natural sleep has been sporadically utilized by artists, mathematicians, and creative people at large.

Here is a tremendously valuable tool of self-hypnosis that you can create for yourself.

Sleep learning can be done through the use of such devices as the "Dormiphone" and all other similar machines that use a timing mechanism, which starts and stops a tape during the hour following the inception and the hour preceding the termination of natural sleep. A period of training may be necessary to overcome the so-called barrier.

For the student or scholar wishing to put "George" to work during his or her natural sleep hours, there may be a few days, or even weeks, without any results.

By repetition of the suggestion, however, the barrier *will* be overcome and results will be seen.

They may be, at first, mere fragments of the sleeping time actually "devoted" by the subconscious mind to the task assigned to it by the presleep suggestion.

With the proper persistence, nevertheless, the time will come when the sleeper can count on a full-night benefit of "inner rumbling" of the thinking machine.

Ideally, the period of natural sleep should be used to review the material you have been exposed to during the period of the same day, so that the "nocturnal reviewing" processes the material absorbed—but not yet digested—during the day.

Because of the special aspect of this suggestion, we would advise the student to use either the "tape," the "folded-paper," or the "pre-blueprinting" techniques of posthypnotic suggestions as they are given here.

To make things easier for the user, we will give in detail each of these three applicable suggestions.

Exercise Number 26A: Sleep Learning Without Machines

Pre-Blueprinting PHS Technique

This suggestion should be self-administered at the moment before going to sleep for the night.

Now, I am going to sleep, hypnotically, at the count of one to twenty and my hypnotic sleep will, within two minutes, transform itself into natural sleep.

I will sleep until such-and-such an hour tomorrow morning. During my natural sleep, my subconscious mind will work at reviewing the classes of this day (or such-and-such material).

The folded-paper technique of PHS could use the same text.

Exercise Number 26: Sleep Learning Without Machines

The Tape Recorder Technique

This is the way the consulting hypnotist might phrase the appropriate suggestion:

Now, whenever you go to sleep at night, you say to yourself, "During this coming night, my mind will be working on such-and-such material . . ."; you then count to twenty and you will automatically go into hypnotic sleep and, within the next two minutes, your hypnotic sleep will transform itself into natural sleep. Then, without disturbing the recuperative value of your natural sleep, your subconscious mind will review the material you have given it to work on, just as if you actually did the mental work in the waking state, and you will wake up in the morning feeling refreshed as usual and recuperated, but you will actually have the benefit of your mind's doing a full and free night shift of working on that material.

Now, I repeat that suggestion (start from beginning, once).

Useful Unused Time

That third of your life that is devoted to sleep could just as easily be used to reinforce any positive suggestion you are working on at the time.

Such a suggestion could be one concerning concentration, memory, discipline, and so on.

Of course, this chapter is obviously devoted to those students and scholars who want to use self-hypnosis "to the limit," but it is nevertheless included here because even if only one or two students, out of the many who use this book, have the natural talent for self-hypnosis, who can tell how far he or she may go?

This is one instance where, truly, the sky is the limit.

CHAPTER 10

Operation "No Jitters'

A Useless Waste Maker

Many more exams and recitations have been failures because of a simple case of the jitters than because of actual ignorance of the subject matter.

That well-known phenomenon, akin to stage fright—with its accompanying symptoms of wobbling knees, parched throat, sweaty palms and other symptoms of mental dissociations—has many facets. It covers the whole gamut from the blank memory to the blank expression of the face.

Some of its victims would be unable to express the reasons for the tremors that take possession of their bodies and minds when it does "take hold of them."

To some, it seems that the examining board has somehow fished out of the blue questions that were never discussed during the academic year; to others, it is merely a vague sensation of void in the upper region of the body, commonly called the head, and to still others it is simply an impression of "nervousness," "not being wholly there," or general uneasiness.

To some of the victims, it is simply the well-deserved realization that the beginning and the end of the academic year have quite suddenly joined one another, and that nothing much has been accomplished—by them—in between the two.

To most of them however, the pangs of conscience are entirely out of order, because they have dutifully used the time during the interim period.

To these latter students especially, self-hypnosis can be very helpful in eliminating those obstacles crucial to the free expression of their knowledge and their worth.

Self-hypnosis is not a miraculous lifesaver. Time wasters should not think that a last-ditch hypnotic miracle will save them from the impending disaster.

Hypnotic or self-hypnotic training or suggestion under the pressure of a deadline, in the vast majority of cases, cannot and should not be considered for two reasons.

First, because the training itself should not be done or undertaken "in extremis"; training in hypnosis or self-hypnosis should first be done in a neutral setting, merely and exclusively for the purpose of acquiring self-hypnosis.

Second, and more important for the matter at hand, posthypnotic suggestions obey an as yet unestablished pattern of efficiency.

Posthypnotic suggestions, whether self- or hetero-administered, can and do take effect according to one of the following patterns:

A daily slight improvement.

Nothing at all for a few days and then,

sudden dramatic effects, with another
period of stagnation.

Slight periodical (not daily) improvement
with increasing frequency.

Initial period of long stagnation and then
setting in of one of the previously mentioned patterns.

Generally, the first pattern of "daily slight
improvement" is the rule, the daily improvement
varying from 1, 2, or 3 percent, or even 5 percent.

The strategy therefore is to be prepared, and
preparedness should be the password of all students. After all, if a person cannot be prepared
as a student, how can he or she expect to be
prepared as a professional?

Reasons for the Jitters

All of the previously mentioned obstacles to
success—wish to fail, spite, preconditionings,
and so on—can be invoked as subconscious
factors of the jitters that assail students in the
exam room.

However, those factors should have been eliminated by now—regularly and systematically—by
the "cloud and sun" or the "burning of the
leaves" exercises.

Nevertheless, there are perfectly natural ex-
planations for that severe type of stage fright
that confronts the examinee to a written or oral
examination.

The solemnity of the setting, the importance
of the occasion to the subject's future, the thousand and one preconditionings from hearsay,
and the reciprocal suggestions of the tense faces
of the unprepared candidates, all are some of
the normal causes of the jitters.

The keynote of the suggestions aimed at dispelling the feelings of anxiety, nervousness, inadequacy, or despondency (which all partly describe the phenomenon) should be relaxation, self-confidence, and self-possession.

Two suggestions will be given here to condition yourself to passing an exam—written or oral—or to presenting a recitation with calm, self-assurance, relaxed mind and body and, consequently, efficiency.

Exercise Number 27: Operation "No Jitters"

Now, we want to suggest to the subconscious mind something very interesting regarding your new behavior during any exam session, and any instance when you have to recall and express your knowledge of subject matters. In the future, and beginning now, whenever you say to yourself: "Now, relaxation until such and such a time . . .," you will feel an extraordinary sense of calm, confidence, and self-possession.

Your mind will be at ease, will function with clarity and poise, and you will feel more calm and cool, as a matter of fact, than in any other circumstances of life. This calm self-confidence and relaxation will be due to many supporting feelings.

It will be supported by the knowledge that you have studied, reviewed, and recapitulated your material.

It will be partly a consequence of the knowledge that whatever you have read, studied, or observed is never erased from your memory bank and that, even without any effort other than that of having attended the necessary classes, almost anyone should be able to remember at least 50 percent of them.

That calm and relaxed feeling will also be partly due to the confidence that you have mentally rehearsed the material by doing some mental shadow questioning on the subject matter you are being tested on.

That same calm relaxed attitude will also instantly come to you when you have to do some recitation or pass any oral examinations. Now, at the count of Three, I want you to see yourself, over and over again, under all kinds of circumstances where you previously would have felt nervous, enjoying feelings of alert relaxation, calm and clear poise of mind and body, as soon as you think to yourself: "Now, relaxation till such-and-such a time . . ."

And during the X minutes that this exercise will require, I want you to see yourself calm and relaxed and alert and poised and as soon as you use the key for producing those feelings—over and over again, for just as long as it would take for the subconscious to produce them automatically upon the elicitation of the signal and for the conscious mind to use them automatically wherever and whenever the circumstances demand it.

One, Two, Three . . .

Note: *By using the L-K-U or the tape PHS techniques, the student will so condition himself or herself to the instantaneous and automatic production of the desired feelings, well before examination* *time, as to feel absolutely secure about their mechanical reiteration by the subconscious mind, when needed.*

As the *alert relaxation* conditioning is gradually learned and tested before its direct needs are met, the student can work leisurely at making it just as complete as he or she wishes it to be in actual life.

Of course, such an exercise can be extended to undoing any reluctance or antipathy to public speech, again by being tested under gradually increased difficulties and reinforced appropriately, according to the evidence of the acquired results.

CHAPTER 11

Mental Imagery: The Tool of Photographic Memory

Parting of the Roads

This chapter may quite reasonably mark the parting of the roads for two groups of readers. Those who have not yet developed—in the course of their training in self-hypnosis—the art of mental visualization, although capable of receiving the full benefits of self-hypnosis in the previously provided techniques, may want to stop here.

This and the following chapters are devoted to higher aspects of self-hypnosis: Their use can "magnify" a person by developing the essential tool of mental imagery.

Those who stop here will probably do so not because of an inherent incapacity to attain mental visualization, but because of the common belief that it is difficult to acquire it.

It is hoped, in all cases, that the student will go on with the perusal of this chapter, if for no other purpose than to find what he or she is missing by not "really going through with it."

But, we repeat, if you are to "drop out" now, by all means read these last two chapters in order to get at least an idea of the possibilities offered.

We continue on to the matter at hand—training in mental imagery.

Pictorial Thinking

The fact that one picture is worth ten thousand words has been appreciated for thousands of years, long before man could write or even speak.

The first thinking of man was done in mental pictures, just as his first writing was done in pictorial designs on the caves of Altamira or elsewhere.

Mental imagining, the making of mental pictures of the outside world, has therefore been a phylogenetic property of man throughout the ages; even the Greek word for *idea* was initially the word for *image*.

Thinking in images, seeing things with your eyes closed, is therefore one of the most natural and the most inevitable inheritances of your very nature.

In order to lose that natural faculty to see things with your eyes closed it takes, just as in *South Pacific*, a lot of contrary conditioning: you must be taught, you must be very carefully taught.

That natural attribute explains the instinctive imagery and poetry of all primitive languages, as is the case with the American Indians.

Speaking and writing have been the first two

of the "extensions of man" so successfully elaborated upon by McLuhan, but, like all other extensions of man, they have partially amputated him of the faculty extended, namely the natural process of thinking in images.

Nevertheless, the faculty still survives and is only gradually lost after birth.

Free Cartoons

Take any child between the ages of six and eleven or even twelve, tell him or her to close his or her eyes because you will "place your thumb on a magical spot between the eyes and then count to seven . . . and, at the count of seven, they will see a very funny cartoon."

Then, place your thumb on the bridge of the child's nose, dutifully count to seven, and watch for the wide, amused grin of the child.

It will happen 99 percent of the time, once you have established your "magical powers" with the child.

Although the figures we will now give are not supported by statistics, but merely the experience of the author, they can readily be confirmed by your own experience and a few days of inquiry in your surroundings.

Approximately 90 percent of all children under thirteen, 50 percent of women of all ages and 25 percent of men of all ages can "close their eyes and see a given object."

As the process of thinking in symbols (words and numbers, spoken or written) becomes more and more a part of our mental processes, the natural faculty of mental imagery gradually wanes and, in some cases, disappears.

The object of this chapter is to train you,

through self-hypnosis, to recapture that natural gift and then use it for learning the specialized techniques of self-hypnosis it permits:

> Training in acquiring a photographic memory.
>
> Time distortion for studying in accelerated time.
>
> Making your professors work overtime by the use of mental hallucination and time distortions.

Those techniques are the tools that will allow you to cut in half the time necessary to absorb a given amount of information or subject matter or double the amount absorbed in the same time.

And that factor, that constant of multiplication of your efficiency at absorbing amounts of learning, can probably be increased to three.

For those who intended to drop out at the last chapter, such a consideration may likely be reason enough to reconsider.

The Steps to a Photographic Memory

Photographic memory comes naturally to a few privileged people. I recall the case of a professional who deplored, at age 72, the fact that "I now have to read a page of Greek twice before I can remember it by heart."

Such a person might be surprised to learn that not everyone possesses such a natural gift, so strong is the disposition in people to take their own case as the universal rule.

Similarly, people who do have the faculty of mental imagining may find it hard to believe that some people do not possess it; and to such as do not possess the capacity to make mental images of whatever they see around them, it may sound unbelievable to hear that they, as well as everybody else, can acquire the power.

To some, it is merely a case of reawakening a natural process of the mind; to others, it may prove rather difficult to learn. But they may be assured that they *do* have it as a natural and innate capacity and they *will* develop it if they stick with it long and hard enough.

Of course, motivation toward the acquisition of the faculty can be enhanced by using all previous tools of self-hypnosis that do not require it.

The necessary steps to a photographic memory are:

1. Mental visualization
2. Proper training and
3. Practice

According to whether you do or do not possess the ability to do some mental imagining—"seeing things with your eyes closed, just as vividly as if you were seeing them on a kind of mental screen, instead of just imagining them"—you will follow the instructions given for Group A or B.

Those who possess the faculty of making clear mental images of things we will call Group A: those who do not possess it we will call Group B.

Training for Group B: The Nonvisualizers

After you have successfully terminated the exercises given in this and the following section of this chapter, you will be ready to join the students of Group A.

The biggest hurdle the nonvisualizer will have to surmount is the "barrier of disbelief."

No matter how easily the similarity can be grasped between "mental imagery" and the nightly process of dreaming, there still persists the vague notion that, somehow, there is some difference between the two.

The hardest obstacle will have been cleared when you can be sure that you have "seen something" with your eyes closed, no matter what that "something" may be.

Even if that "something" is just a hazy, muddled mass of dark and darker shades—or some nebulous black and gray color—as soon as you can discern some pattern of organization, you will then and there know that "I can do it, too."

Of course, as you reach this chapter, it is assumed that you have, as indicated, passed the tests of each previous chapter. In other words, it is assumed that:

1. You possess self-hypnosis.
2. You can "go under" for a specified number of minutes.
3. You have tested your hypnotic state by some simple posthypnotic suggestion, even if it is nothing else but the compulsion to pick up a book or shouting "Hallelujah" once you have come out of the hypnotic state.
4. You have already practiced posthypnotic suggestions (such as those concerning concentration, memory, or reviewing after reading) and experienced the effects thereof in the waking state.

Only if you have accomplished those preliminary tests of self-hypnosis should you have come thus far anyway.

If not, what are you doing here?

Assuming you have fulfilled the required conditions as outlined, let us now proceed with the techniques that will save you time in acquiring *Mental Visualization*.

Acquiring Mental Visualization

The first requisite, after that of being already adept in self-hypnosis, will be to learn a new type of timed hypnosis.

The exercises that will train you in acquiring the art of seeing things or objects mentally, as if they were projected onto a mental internal screen, should be timed as follows:

"Until I have seen such-and-such a thing or until five minutes are elapsed, whichever happens first."

Once the "thing" that is the object of the exercise has been "seen," the exercise, for all intents and purposes, is over and should be terminated.

So, the exercises aiming at acquiring mental imagery should be programmed as follows:

You *blueprint* the exercise before you do it. The blueprint says: "Now I will sleep for so many minutes or until I have seen such-and-such a thing, whichever happens first.

Now, the thing I want to visualize is . . ."

And then, you use your self-hypnotic key, naturally consisting of counting from one to twenty.

The something to be seen could be something or some color, something or some concrete object, in general, without specification.

The first exercise is outlined here so that everything will be perfectly clear in the mind of the student.

Exercise Number 28: Let Me See Something

Now, I will go to sleep for five minutes, or until I have seen something.

Whichever happens first. I will then wake up feeling fine and refreshed. Now, that something may be a concrete object, it may be some color, even if only an undefined splotch of color. One, Two, Three . . .

Note: *This is a turning point in your hypnotic training because you are a nonvisualizer.*

It may happen quite naturally that you will "see" nothing for quite a few sessions of five minutes and that you will then, suddenly, see a fleeting image of "something" projecting itself onto the screen of your mind.

Sooner or later, some image is going to form itself on that screen and then, the hurdle is gone: You will *know* that you can do it, like everybody else.

Some have found it more profitable to use sessions of fifteen minutes or thirty minutes at the start.

Some have found it expedient to "talk to George."

Some have decided that regular, impatience-free sessions of five minutes at a time, in series of three, have given them the impression that they were gradually "imagining" things better and more clearly.

If color should come first, you may play at having that color move or form a given or un-specified shape, but do not for a moment believe that there should be anything compulsory or sacred about color.

The object is to achieve the mental visualization of some "object," some concrete object, such as a chair, a telegraph post, or a pencil.

Color is totally unimportant; it is suggested simply because some psychologist and physiologists have found some reason for believing that colors should be easier to produce as mental images.

Afterimage

You may find some facilitation of your task in using the afterimage, which is the image that remains in the eye for a fraction of a second after you have looked at a given object for a few seconds.

In order to render this afterimage more efficient, you may fix your gaze on a given object for as long as two, three, or even five or ten minutes and then close your eyes.

Quite evidently, as soon as you close your eyes, it becomes rather easy to visualize mentally the same object that you have been fixating for such a long time.

This technique is in fact given to people undertaking some Yoga practices and can be used quite advantageously for training yourself in mental visualization.

If "your case" is rather difficult, a few days or weeks of such training in afterimage evocation will be very helpful.

The practice consists simply of training yourself, in all possible moments of leisure, at fixating objects in your immediate surroundings and then closing your eyes and "trying" to "re-see" them mentally.

Inevitably, you will find that, every day, in some mysterious way, you are getting better and better at doing just that thing.

Once you have succeeded at seeing some concrete object, no matter what that object may be—chair, baseball bat, or angel—you there and then belong to Group A. You can now continue with the exercise of the next paragraph.

And you will *never* regret whatever time and effort you may have spent on the subject.

Exercise Number 29: Developing Mental Visualization

For Groups A and B

This is a whole series of exercises aimed at developing the clarity, immediacy, and "staying-put" quality of the mental images.

It is a series of "five minutes or until objective attained exercises," in which the blueprint contains the mental stipulation that the subject will "come back to normal" as soon as the five minutes have elapsed or the "thing to be visualized" has actually been *seen* on the inner screen of the mind.

Quite obviously, when the exercise aims at

holding a given image, the alternative termina-
tions will not apply and the exercise should be
carried on for the predetermined number of
minutes—namely, two, three, four, or five minutes.

Here is the list of exercises that should be
practiced in the order given, with the appropriate blueprint self-administered before the self-
hypnotic key is used.

Each objective additionally should constitute
the objective of one and only one exercise:

> Let me see a series of concrete objects.

> Let me see such-and-such a concrete
> object.

> Let me see some abstract object.

An abstract object evidently will not be an
abstract object, which, by definition, does not
exist in the realm of physical things, such as
Beauty, Strength, Health, Peace, War, Friend-
ship, Love, Calm and so on.

For the needs of these exercises, an abstract
object will be some concrete image, an arche-
type or a conventional or personal substitute
for the abstract concept demanded. For example, Peace may be seen as the universally known
dove, or some peaceful scenery already stocked
in the memory bank of the subject or made
afresh by the imagination at the time of the
exercise.

> Let me see such-and-such an abstract
> object.

Chosen from the preceding list or under the
"inspiration" of the moment, that inspiration
naturally translating a natural and subconscious
preference for the image chosen at the time:

> Let me see a blackboard.

> Let me see a television set.

> Let me see some "neutral person."

Some person with whom you have no negative or especially positive relation, such as your mail carrier or your UPS or paper delivery person.

Let me see some person.

Neutral or not, that is, and this may be your mother-in-law, your professor, your friend (of either sex), your football coach and so on

Let me see such-and-such a person.

Let me see letter A, or R, or some other letter.

That letter could be standing in thin air or written on a blackboard, and you may then pass on to the whole alphabet, one letter per exercise or the whole sequence of the alphabet, from A to Z, or from A to Z and then back again to A in one exercise.

Let me see some two-letter word.

Let me see some three-letter word.

Let me see some four-letter word.

Let me see such-and-such a word.

Let me see a stage, curtains drawn or closed.

Note: *Do not let yourself become "stuck" on such-and-such an image, which somehow seems to be difficult to imagine; pass on to some other exercise and forget that obstinate image. You are merely training yourself in mental imagery and you do not have time to analyze the possible subconcious blocks or resistances to such-and-such an image.*

Exercise Number 30: Training for a Photographic Memory

This again is given, and for obvious reasons, as a series of mental self-hypnotic exercises.

Take a newspaper, scan it for the headlines for a few minutes, and then do the following exercises:

> Let me see the first two words of that same headline.
>
> Let me see the whole headline.
>
> Let me see some illustration I have seen in that paper.

If necessary look again at that picture and then do the exercise once more.

Take a book, look at the title page, and then do the exercise:

> Let me see the title page of that book.

Now, read a full paragraph, two or three times, from that book and do the following exercise:

> Let me see the first half of the first line of that paragraph.
>
> Let me see the whole of the first line of that paragraph.

Or, after looking at it for a few seconds,

> Let me see such-and-such a chart from that book, then,
>
> Let me see the whole of such and such a paragraph.

And then:

> After you mastered one whole paragraph, you can pass on to *two* paragraphs.

Daily mental practice on the headlines, on charts, and pictures from books and/or papers will sharpen your mental eyes.

Note: *The purpose of a photographic memory is not, in the context of this book, that of becoming able to "read a page of text once and then know it by heart," no matter how dramatic and showy the feat might seem; it is instead the faculty of mentally photocopying important elements of written information that one may need to use at any given moment.*

As a matter of fact, with the proper training, a student can rather easily, at exam time, copy from the book a certain text with impunity, because the copying is done in the mind.

A rather interesting method of training your mental imagery can be used to perfect the ability while entertaining yourself. It consists of undergoing hypnosis for a given number of minutes while a piece of music is played and after having ordered the subconscious mind to "translate" the given piece of music into images and thus producing your own Disney-like *Fantasia.*

Obviously, no amount of skill in photographic memory will replace the *understanding* of your subject matter.

One can appreciate, however, how valuable it can be to the student of law or architecture and so on.

Helpful Advice

It is obvious that the acquisition and perfecting of a photographic memory are serious matters. Once in possession of such a faculty, the user will find innumerable advantages for it and would certainly not exchange it for "a pot of lentils."

Because this is a very serious objective it may be worthwhile to note that a basic list of the essentials is as follows:

1. A program of training.
2. A most systematic and constant use of the tool.

A constant facilitation of the processes of visualization and continuous improvement of image recall will result from the endeavor, as well as the persistent flow of "discoveries" about its possible applications.

Because of the time and energy involved, it may be wise to acquire immediately "some" measure of photographic memory and pass on to the uses of self-hypnosis given in the next chapter, making a reasonable facsimile of a true photographic memory a long-range goal.

CHAPTER 12

Studying on the Triple

Time Distortion in the Waking Life

Subjective time, the time that seems necessary for a given fraction of life (event or episode) to take place, is an elastic quantity that can be compressed or expanded, generally under uncontrollable factors.

Numerous expressions of the common usage illustrate our perception of that "experiential time" being different from the usual clock time: "How time flies in good company"; "Happy days are short days"; "It seemed like a lifetime" are all common wordings of the fact that we sense time to be different subjectively from what it is objectively.

Let us suppose that two observers, at the same time but in two different halls, each attend a fifteen-minute session conducted by two different speakers. One lecture concerns the extrapolation of metaphysics from anthropological data, the other is a "comedy show" given by a well-known entertainer.

Let us suppose that neither observer took note of the clock time spent by each lecturer. Then, let us ask each one of those observers the question: "How long did it last?"

Of course, in each case, the answer to this first question would be something like: "I don't know; I didn't take note of the time."

Now, let us ask each subject the following question: "How long did it *seem* to last?" Naturally—as you have already anticipated—the subjects will answer differently.

The one who has attended the conference on metaphysics, unless he is a real enthusiast of the subject matter, will answer: "It seemed to me to last about twenty-five minutes," whereas the person who attended the comedy show will answer: "Well, I wish it had been longer; in fact, it seemed to last about ten minutes."

Such is our subjective time, which we have already called "experiential time"; it is a personally estimated duration that varies according to the circumstances under which the given experience has been lived; it is a *seeming* duration.

There are therefore both a "real" or clock time and an "apparent" time.

Under excessive fatigue or the stunning influence of a highly captivating event (airplane catastrophe, automobile accident, the shock of a loved one's death, etc.), objective time suddenly takes a turn for the worse or at least for the different; it seems to "stand still" (as in ecstasy) or it seems to "go like a flash."

One subject has related how, while on the last stretch of a long automobile journey, after having driven for eight hours and feeling "some" fatigue, he suddenly had a strange feeling of "slow motion" as he was driving at the approximate speed of seventy-five miles an hour.

It seemed to him that "that was no speed at all," that the motion of his car seemed so slow that he felt he could take time to look around at leisure and he thought he could have ridden at twice the speed without feeling it. He even remembered saying to himself; "Man, if this is speed, give me more of it, and lots more."

Time distortion in the waking state, although certainly not under ordinary circumstances, is said to attain extraordinary proportions in the case of the drowning person who sees his entire life unwind in a flash in his mind.

Time Distortion Under Hypnosis

Time distortion is a natural concomitant of hypnosis. After a one-hour session, during which a person "slept" most of the time, the subject to whom you ask the question, "How long do you think you were asleep," is likely to make a tentative answer such as: "About twenty minutes?"

In most hypnotic situations, time (i.e., experiential time) is compressed, like hay in a bale: the time it *seems* to "live" a certain hallucinated or mentally relived sequence of past life is *longer* than the clock time it took to see it under hypnosis.

It is quite aptly compared with the experience of dreams, in which things that would take hours or even days to live can be "relived" within a few seconds or minutes.

Cases are not rare in which a subject has "seen," during the clock time of *ten seconds*, the whole of a long film such as *Gone With the Wind*.

In hypnotic and self-hypnotic-training, however, the purpose is to control time distortion and produce it at will instead of waiting for its spontaneous happening under unforeseen and unforeseeable factors.

Before going any further in this chapter, to let you know what time distortion is and thus be more skilled in grasping its concomitants, which are described later, it has seemed best to propose the following exercise.

Exercise Number 31: An Experiment in Distorted Time

You are by now sufficiently trained in self-hypnosis to perform quite successfully the following experiment in time distortion. Because of your acquired skill in self-posthypnotic suggestions we will merely give the blueprint to be used.

Now the object of this hypnotic period is the "reliving" of some episode of frequent occurrence in your daily life. Quite naturally, the specific sequence of events given may not be directly applicable to your own life, and you should alter the text to fit your own circumstances.

Blueprint

Now I want to sleep until the reliving of this sequence of happenings is over, starting at the last count of one to twenty.

Now, let me relive my daily walk from the classroom, through the campus grounds and back to the classroom, after having browsed in the bookstore, as I do in fact every day. When the whole walk to and fro is over, let me wake up. (Note the time on your watch.)

One, Two, Three . . .

After waking up, note the time and establish the following mathematical ratio: the time it seemed to take (which is the same time it actually takes you to do that walk daily) divided by the clock or watch reading:

$$\frac{\text{Experiential time}}{\text{Clock time}} = \text{Distortion Ratio}$$

This experiment will have acquainted you with the following data about time distortion:

You have no impression of rushing or being rushed. In fact, you do have all the time in the world, like you would have—and feel to have—if you did the thing in "real life" once more.

You wake up to find that the clock time has been inferior to the factually "required clock time" to perform the same series of actions.

The "usually required clock time" is the time you seem to have at your disposal; it is experiential time, alias subjective time, alias apparent time.

Note: *In cases like the preceding one in which the prehypnotic suggestion is to perform an* allotted *task, there is no direct suggestion for time distortion; the experiment therefore gives you a direct example of time distortion as a concomitant to*

*hypnosis. And you can readily perceive
the notion of time distortion ratio as being
the mathematical ratio. In this case:*

Actual and usual time of allotted task time to relive under hypnosis

In the same fashion, one could relive a class session, *once*, by using a fraction of the time it actually took to attend the class.

It can then quite naturally be inferred that, by using a "repeated allotted task" formula, one can "reattend" a given class a number of times during a short period of clock time, which is the title of this chapter.

Studying on the triple means that a time distortion ratio of *three-to-one* has been achieved.

In this chapter we will equip you with a ten-to-one time-distortion ratio.

The Value of Time Distortion

The important fact about this method of practicing time distortion is that such mental reviewing, whether applied to an artistic or athletic performance, or to a learning session, has almost the same effect as the actual repeated performance in fact and in regular clock time.

Musicians, using such a method by "practicing" on their instrument during such hallucinatory time-distorted hypnotic sessions, have acquired the corresponding and factual facilitation of the hallucinated performance.

Difficult passages have become "easy as pie," long pieces have been learned by heart, and the performances of them rendered automatic through automatic muscle memory, the naturalness, expressivity, and artistic level of renditions have been increased, and so on.

Physiologists have demonstrated that miniaturized but real nerve impulses do in fact reach the appropriate muscles *during* the hypnotic session and the repeated reactivation of the neural paths has been responsible for the results obtained by musicians, performing artists, and even athletes.

Instead of the usual pep talk before a football game, some athletes have used a short session of "mentally seeing themselves functioning ideally during the game," and experience has proven that the results thus obtained surpassed those of a control group of athletes using the standard impetus of a good pep talk from the coach.

Purpose of This Chapter

It becomes quite evident that the use of time distortion can be an invaluable tool for a student.

The purpose of this chapter is twofold:

1. Training you in hypnotic time distortion.
2. Equipping you with some of its applied techniques for the art of learning.

Exercise Number 32: Training in Time Distortion

Because numerous cases have been witnessed in which a "natural" increase in the ratio of time distortion has occurred by the mere fact of repeating the exercises, without any specific efforts toward acceleration, it is suggested that the following list of exercises be practiced.

They all consist is *reliving once* a well-known task.

They all follow the "allotted-task" formula already used in the previous exercise of this chapter; in other words, the exercise is over when the hallucinated task is over in the mental machine.

Procedure

In each case, the blueprint is:
> Now, let me sleep until I have relived,
> Once, the following task, namely . . .
> Note time and use self-hypnotic key:
> One . . .

Keeping Tabs

In each case, take note of the time distortion obtained for future reference.
> Use a pad and keep it handy for each session. Inscribe the date, the nature of the task, the time it would take to actually do the task, and the clock time necessary to relive the hypnotic exercise.
> Be sure to enter the *ratio* of time distortion.

Allotted Tasks

>   Some regular car ride.
>   A familiar walk in town.
>   The events of the previous day.
>   A recently attended class.
>   A well-liked play.
>   A well-known film.
>   A recent sports event one has attended.

Having done the previous exercises once, one could do the whole list over again once, but we suggest the following:

>   Do the whole list over again, but relive each item three times in succession instead of just once—and keep tabs.

Having acquainted yourself with time distortion by these exercises and having already established some distortion ratio, you may use the following exercise, which is an example of the suggestion a hypnotist would use for training a subject in the art.

You may or may not do this exercise, which is presented to give you some additional information on the phenomenon.

Time Distortion Suggested

Now, presently, I am going to count to three and when I have finished the count, you will begin to see yourself counting pennies. At the count of three, you will be in a hall where you will find a large table, with the sides bordered by a ledge and, in the center of that table, a huge heap of pennies.

You will be at the spot at the table and you

will begin to count the pennies, in lots of fifty, then roll the stack into the paper holder, neatly stacking the ends, and put the rolled lot of pennies aside. Then, you will count another fifty, roll it up, and stack it with the previous bundle.

You will *feel* that you are thus counting pennies and stacking them up in bundles for a full hour.

You won't feel rushed in any fashion and you will have all the time necessary to do the job neatly and accurately.

When the time seems to have lasted one full hour, you will wake up, feeling fine and refreshed, and you will remember everything very clearly.

One, Two, Three . . .

This suggestion has been couched as an "allotted-time" exercise; that is, the subject has been given "one full hour of apparent time" to do a given task.

When he does "wake up," the operator will note the time elapsed since he counted to three, which was the starting signal, and establish therefrom the ratio of time distortion obtained.

Another type of exercise is the one in which the subject is given or gives himself a certain quantity of clock time in which to do a number of tasks of known required factual time or in which to repeat a certain task a given number of times.

Allotted Clock-Time Suggestion

In this formula, the hypnotist would word his or her suggestion along these lines.

Now, we all know that there are two kinds of time; there is the actual, factual time which is measured by the displacement of the hands of the clock, and there is also the apparent subjective time, which is the seeming duration of the events or series of events we live.

In a dream, for instance, one can live within a matter of seconds or minutes things that would take hours or even days to live. Now, when I count to three, you will sleep for five minutes of clock time, you will sleep for five minutes by my watch, but it will *seem* to last much longer than five minutes; in fact, it will seem to last much more like an hour or so.

During that apparent hour, you will be counting apples (text analogous to preceding suggestion).

You won't feel rushed in any fashion, and so on.

One, Two, Three . . .

This method has the advantage that one can suggest afterward that "this time, the apparent time will seem yet longer, even though you will only sleep *five minutes* of actual time by my watch . . . the time distortion will be greater . . .," because the concept of time distortion is now clear in the trainee's mind.

Increasing Time-Distortion Ratio

The first requirement for increasing the ratio of time distortion is practice. It can also be enhanced by direct suggestion.

We will therefore include a second series of suggested exercises for training yourself in time distortion and then provide a direct suggestion for increasing the distortion ratio.

Exercise Number 33: More Training in Time Distortion

Sequence of Allotted Tasks

This is an "until over" suggestion.

Instead of doing one task three times, as in the previous series of exercises, one does a sequence of two or three different tasks, starting at the count of three and the hypnosis ending "when the tasks are over."

Because the student is already familiar with this type of exercise, we will suggest only a few sequences of "tasks" to be performed under hypnosis.

> Having a good meal, having a haircut and visiting a friend.
>
> Attending a sporting event, taking a walk in town, and making a stop at the coffee shop.
>
> Attending a class, studying for twenty minutes and going to a restaurant for a soda.

Repetition of Given Task in Allotted Clock Time

This is enjoying much apparent time in five minutes of clock time.

Therefore, the exercises in this series consist in putting yourself to sleep and pre-blueprinting the task to be performed during those five minutes, without being rushed in any fashion, as many repetitions of a given task, thereby "forcing" the subconscious mind to perform a given ratio of time distortion.

Here are a few possibilities.

> I will relive four times X pleasant moment of my life.
>
> I will see three times that last class in psychology.
>
> Let me do an hour's worth of practicing dunk shots.
>
> Let me recap five times such-and-such a chapter of my book on history.

Allotted Apparent Time

Where an activity is continuous, one may use the "allotted apparent time" formula, in which the suggestion is that "you will be doing such-and-such a thing, for a time which will seem like an hour or thirty minutes or two hours, beginning with the starting signal One, Two, Three . . . and you will wake up when it seems to have lasted an hour, and so on."

Direct Suggestions for Increasing Ratio

Again, we only give the formulation the hypnotist would use in actual practice, and from which the student will derive the application to his or her own preferred method of PHS.

Now, whenever you practice time distortion, you will find the ratio of apparent time to clock time is each time increasing and you are getting each time nearer and nearer to the *ten*-to-*one* ratio, which you may have set as a target. Each time, the imaging is clearer and more "real" and whenever you apply it to studying, you get the same benefit as you would if you actually studied or reviewed your material just as long in reality as the time appears to be under hypnosis.

Applications

The student has had in this chapter ample occasion to consider the possible applications of time distortion to his or her studies.

Reviewing a class just as soon as possible after it has been attended, under hypnosis and in distorted time, will become an invaluable asset.

Reviewing the classes of the day at the end of the day while using a time distortion ratio of ten-to-one can save precious time and offer possibilities for study, which would be impossible to obtain from the scant twenty-four hours of clock time one has been allotted for each day.

Reviewing (reading over and over under hypnosis) a chapter of a textbook is eminently adapted to time distortion.

And, in order to prime your creativity into finding your own applications, may we suggest:

> Having your professor work overtime for you by having him or her repeat three, four, six, or ten times a lecture (not necessarily given in real life) on an ambiguous point, on a whole chapter, on the questions that might appear on exams, and so on.
>
> Improving some artistic skill, such as violin or piano or painting.
>
> Improving your putting or driving by doing the ideal thing under time distortion.
>
> Improving your skill as an actor, as a speaker, as a singer.
>
> Perfecting your memorization of a piece of music, and so on.

You now have the tool.

Use it regularly and find new uses for it.

For referral to certified hypnotists/hypnotherapists and approved hypnotism schools write to:

> Hypnotist's Examining Council
> 1922 Westwood Boulevard, Dept. P
> Los Angeles, CA 90025

For catalog of hypnosis motivation and programming cassettes, write to:

> Westwood Publishing Company
> 1922-D Westwood Boulevard
> Los Angeles, CA 90025

About the Author

In more than thirty-five years of clinical practice, Pierre Clement achieved a reputation for his use of hypnotherapy as a dramatically rapid behavior modification process. His School of Hypnotism in San Francisco was the training ground for many of America's best-known practitioners of hypnosis.

Signet Supernatural

Buy them at your local

bookstore or use coupon

on next page for ordering.